THE MAN WHO DIED FOR ME

Other books by Herbert Lockyer

All About Bible Study
All the Men of the Bible
The Women of the Bible
All the Miracles of the Bible
All the Parables of the Bible
All the Prayers of the Bible
All the Doctrines of the Bible
All the Kings and Queens of the Bible
All the Children of the Bible
All the Promises of the Bible
All the Books and Chapters of the Bible
All the Holy Days and Holidays
All the Trades and Occupations of the Bible
All the Apostles of the Bible
All the Messianic Prophecies of the Bible
All the Divine Names and Titles of the Bible
The Funeral Sourcebook
The Lenten Sourcebook
The Man Who Changed the World (2 vols.)
The Week That Changed the World
Last Words of Saints and Sinners
The Sins of Saints
The Gospel of the Life Beyond
The Unseen Army
Twin Truths of Scripture (2 vols.)
Triple Truths of Scripture (3 vols.)
How to Find Comfort in the Bible
Seven Words of Love

THE MAN WHO DIED FOR ME

Meditations on the Death

and Resurrection of Our Lord

Herbert Lockyer

Blest Cross! Blest Sepulchre!
Blest rather be, the Man
That there, was put to shame for me.
John Bunyan

WORD BOOKS
PUBLISHER
4800 WEST WACO DRIVE
WACO, TEXAS
76703

Contents

Introduction

As you will learn as you read the meditations in this book, we still glory in the Cross of Christ, seeing it continues to "tower o'er the wrecks of time," as Sir John Bowring expresses it in his well-known Calvary hymn. It is beyond all doubt and question that the central fact and event of earth history is the day when the God-Man died to redeem a lost world. Since then, more books, poems, and hymns devoted to the Cross have been written than any other theme you care to think of, whether spiritual or secular. More sermons have been preached on "the eclipsing topic of the Cross" than on any other subject of Scripture. Although almost 2,000 years have passed since Jesus died, more people gather at *Easter* services to remember his dying love than at any other calendar event.

H. A. W. Meyer, theologian of the nineteenth century, once wrote, "The propitiation of Christ is the epoch and turning point in the world's history. By the sacrifice of Himself, and by this act alone, are we reconciled to God." From the most appalling scene the world ever witnessed, a paradise of peace sprang forth, and the Cross became the symbol of man's deliverance from the penalty and power of sin. The day Jesus died will remain the most momentous day in the history of earth because it was then that the Cross became heaven's trysting place, where heaven's love and justice met, and righteousness and peace kissed each other.

In his monumental work on *The Suffering Saviour,* F. W. Krummacher says, "The seven words uttered by Jesus on the Cross sound in our ears like the funeral knell of the kingdom of Satan, and like intimations of liberty and joy to the sinful race of man."

Among the almost one hundred books I possess on the *Cross,* the one that always moves me most deeply whenever I return to it is Dr. William Clow's, *The Cross in Christian Experience.* Although written over seventy years ago, it is perennial in its influence. In his book the renowned Scottish preacher has this most impressive paragraph:

"Every religious movement, whether in a single human soul or in a community, which leaves out the Cross, ends like a desert river in a march, or slips into a chill and pallid Unitarianism. . . . In the teaching of Jesus, and especially in the words which He uttered with the solemn appeal that men should let them sink down into their hearts, in the preeminence given to His death, in the preaching of the Apostles, and the appeals of the Epistles, the eclipsing topic is the Cross and its redeeming sacrifice. The great saints, the men and women who have spread abroad Christ's name and hazarded their lives for His sake, whose sanctity has been persuasive Gospel and compelling Epistle, have all stood at the Cross."

So they have—and multitudes today have taken their stand beneath the Cross of Jesus and have found it to be—

> The shadow of a mighty Rock,
>   Within a weary land:
> A home within the wilderness,
>   A rest upon the way,

From the burning of the noontide heat,
And the burdens of the day.
Elizabeth C. Clephane

No sincere searcher for truth has ever failed to discover that the Cross casts its shadow over the whole of Scripture, and, as Sir John Bowring wrote,

All the light of sacred story
Gathers round its head sublime.

A scarlet highway runs through the whole territory of the Bible, which makes it a crimson Book. Threaded all through the rope used by the British Navy is a thin red cord, so that no matter where it is cut into, identity of ownership is immediately established. Thus is it with the Bible: open where you may, you will find the blood-red cord, for it has been sprinkled with blood (Heb. 9:19, 20). The Cross is central both in God's eternal purpose, and in the revelation of himself which his Word affords. The Book and the Cross can be viewed in this comprehensive survey:

IN THE PAST

Although it may sound somewhat confusing, actually Jesus died before he was born, for he came as the Lamb slain from before the foundation of the world. Calvary was no afterthought of God, or even a cruel death perpetrated solely by evil man, but the plan conceived by God in a past eternity. It was then he foreordained that his Son should die as the Savior of the World. It was then that Love drew salvation's plan. When the Trinity counseled as to what must be done after man sinned following his creation, the Father said, "Whom shall I send, and who will go for us?" Immediately God the Son replied, "Here am I; send me!" And in the fulness of time he came, as the Lamb literally slain to take away the sin of the world. Thus, before there was a *sinner,* there was a *Savior.* God provided the remedy before the disease appeared. What the Father, Son, and Spirit conceived in the dateless past, the Son consummated at Calvary (See 1 Cor. 2:7, 8; Eph. 1:4; 1 Peter 1:18–20: Rev. 13:8).

IN PROMISE

Strange though it may seem, the first promise of the Cross was not given to Adam and Eve, the first sinners on earth, but to Satan who caused them to sin. It was he who, disguised as a serpent, first heard the evangel of God's redemption purpose in the promise: The seed of the woman "shall bruise thy head, and thou shalt bruise his heel" (Gen. 3:15). The moment Christ, the seed of the woman, was born, Satan sought to slay him, and he continued his efforts to kill Jesus. He was hellbent on preventing the Cross because he knew from God's initial promise that it would be his *Waterloo.* The supreme mission of the Incarnation was to destroy the works of the devil, which Jesus accomplished as he died crying, "It is finished" (John 20:30; cp. 1 John 3:8). The provision made for sin in eternity and the promise in Eden was perfected at Calvary.

IN PICTURE

The first books of Scripture covering law and history are replete with cameos or types of what transpired when the Man of Sorrows died. Where is there a more soul-moving illustration of the Father-heart of God in the surrender of his Son than that found in Abraham's response to the divine command to sacrifice his only son? Was not this unquestioned obedience the supreme act in Abraham's life? Surely this was the highest reach of human devotedness to the will of God!

But though God asked for the old man's greatest treasure, he never intended to receive it, for he told Abraham that his demand was only meant to test his obedience. So Isaac, the well-loved son of promise, was spared the knife his father was about to drive into him. A substitute was found in the ram caught in the thicket and laid on the altar as a burnt offering in place of Isaac (Gen. 22:1–14). As Abraham gave up his only son to God, God gave *his* only begotten Son, but with this difference: Isaac was not slain by his father's knife, but Jesus met death upon the altar. At Calvary, the knife of divine justice was plunged deep into his loving, holy heart. There was no substitute for him, seeing he died as the sinless Substitute for sinners. God "spared not his own Son, but delivered him up for us all" (Rom. 8:32). Even the substitute found for Isaac, the ram, was a type of Jesus offered as a burnt offering in our place (Heb. 10:5–10). As for Isaac himself, he was no mere child when his father bound him and laid him on the altar. In this he is a striking picture of Jesus "obedient unto death" (Phil. 2:8. See also Num. 21:8, 9).

With the institution of the Levitical order, foreshadowings of the Cross became more evident as the pages of *Leviticus,* dripping with blood, prove. The Holy Spirit summarized the teaching of the offering up of innumerable lambs when he inspired Moses to write, "The life of the flesh is in the blood: and I have given it to you upon the altar to make an atonement for your souls: for it is the blood that maketh an atonement for the soul" (Lev. 17:11). Thus, from Abel's first accepted offering to the last lamb sacrificed under the Law Dispensation, the sacrifice was a pattern of "The Lamb of God, which taketh away the sin of the world" (John 1:29). Then it is not too difficult to see the "line of scarlet thread in the window" as a means of escape, a color-picture of our eternal deliverance and safety through sacrifice (Heb. 9:19, 22).

Not all the blood of beasts,
  On Jewish altars slain,
Could give the guilty conscience peace,
  Or wash away their stain.

But Christ the heavenly Lamb,
  Takes all our sins away;
A sacrifice of nobler Name,
  And richer blood, than they.

Isaac Watts

In Poetry

Biblical poetry, expressive of inner feelings, is both devotional and prophetical. From *Job* we gather these two foregleams of the accomplishment of the Cross. The patriarch, who was a problem to himself, complained that there was no daysman between God and himself who would lay his hand upon both and reconcile them. But a daysman or mediator had been given by God, as the heart of Job came to realize. As Ellicott comments on Job 9:33,

"Job felt, as he had been taught to feel, that in himself there not only was no hope, but no possibility of Justification with God, unless there should be an umpire and impartial mediator, who could make the cause of both his own, and reconcile and unite the two in himself."

How far Job understood his own words we do not know, but they accurately express what God has given us, for at the Cross, Jesus our Daysman laid one hand upon God and the other hand upon the sinner, and brought about reconciliation. "There is one God, and one mediator between God and man, the man Christ Jesus, who gave himself a ransom for all" (1 Tim. 2:5, 6. See Gal. 3:19, 20). Job then goes on to confess that he found in God, the living, eternal Redeemer whom he would one day see (19:25, 26). The word Job used for *Redeemer* was "the name given to the next of kin whose duty it was to redeem, ransom, or avenge one who had fallen into debt or bondage, or had been slain in a family feud." Man was deeply in debt to God, and in bondage to the devil, but Calvary provided the Redeemer who paid the debt and provided deliverance from satanic servitude.

As he died upon the Cross, Jesus quoted the great Messianic Psalm 22. As a later chapter carries a full exposition of this Calvary Psalm, the following observation by Ellicott will suffice at this juncture. "The fact that Jesus uttered from His Cross the words of bitter woe that begins this poem, have given and must ever give it a special interest and importance. It was natural that Christian sentiment should fasten lovingly on it, and almost claim it, not only as a record of suffering typical of our Lord's suffering, but . . . actually in every detail prophetic of Him."

IN PROPHECY

We have our Lord's own authority on the prophetic outlook of the Old Testament regarding his life and death, for he told his disciples, "All things must be fulfilled, which were written in the law of Moses, and in the prophets, and in the psalms, *concerning me*" (Luke 24:44). See also John 12:41, a passage that can be linked to Isaiah 53, which drips with the ruby blood of the Redeemer. In succeeding chapters fuller mention will be made of this wonderful Calvary chapter.

Then who but the Spirit of Revelation could have given to Zechariah the forecast of the dastardly betrayal of Jesus by Judas; and also the solemn truth of the pierced hands of him who, as the Good Shepherd, gave his life for the sheep (11:12, 13; 13:6, 7)? Peter must have had in mind prophets like Isaiah and Zechariah when he wrote that the Holy Spirit within them inspired them to testify "beforehand the sufferings of Christ" (1 Peter 1:11).

IN PERFORMANCE

Because Christ declared that his death upon a Cross was the end for which he was born, the whole of the New Testament is heavy with references to all aspects of his finished work; and further on in these meditations we will consider this phase of our study. The Gospels reveal that Jesus had his death in prospect from the moment when John the Baptist proclaimed him to be the Lamb of God who would bear away the sin of the world. Here are his explicit, anticipatory proclamations:

"The Son of man (shall) be three days and three nights in the heart of the earth" (Matt. 12:40).

"The Son of Man shall be betrayed unto the chief priests and unto the scribes, and they shall condemn him to death . . . crucify him: and the third day he shall rise again" (Matt. 20:18, 19. See Mark 8:31; 9:12).

"If I be lifted up from the earth. . . . this he said signifying what death he should die" (John 12:32, 33).

"Jesus knew that his hour was come that he should depart out of this world unto the Father" (John 13:1).

"This I say unto you, that this that is written must yet be accomplished in me, And he was reckoned among the transgressors: for the things concerning me have an end" (Luke 22:37).

The Pharisees and Herod tried to kill Jesus before his death in the prescribed way. But Jesus emphasized that he was immortal until his work was accomplished in his challenging words to Herod: "Go ye, and tell that fox. . . . I must walk today, and tomorrow, and the day following" (Luke 13:32, 33).

A pertinent truth that must be borne in mind is that Jesus carried no death-seed in himself. We are born to live, yet from our first day in the world we begin our funeral march to the grave. "Born in sin, and shapen in iniquity" (which means being made recipients of original sin at birth), we become sinners by our own volition; and "so death passed upon all men, for all have sinned," and "the wages of sin is death" (Rom. 5:12; 6:23). "In the day thou eatest thereof thou shalt surely die" (Gen. 2:17). "The soul that sinneth it shall die" (Ezek. 18:4, 20). "In Adam all die" (1 Cor. 15:22).

As the result of our acceptance of Jesus as personal Savior, we are delivered from spiritual death by the operation of the Holy Spirit, and from eternal death by the sacrifice of Jesus, but not from *physical death,* which is the earthly end for us all whether saint or sinner. The hope of the saint is that he may be alive when Jesus returns, as he said he would, and that he may have the delight of going to glory without dying. But if he does die, then dying in the Lord, he is blessed.

With Jesus himself, it was totally different, for no inherited death-seed was his. Although born to die (not because of sin, seeing he was sinless and separate from sinners), Jesus did not have the seed of death *in* him. Sinless, he was death-less, and so death, *our death,* came *upon* him. Being without sin, his death was not the death of a sinner, but of a sinless Sacrifice—of a Lamb without blemish and without spot— vicarious, propitiatory, atoning. It was a death satisfying all the just claims of a broken law, appeasing the righteous wrath of an offended God, and paying the full penalty of the sin of the world. Such a death came early, for he died before his prime, being only thirty-three years of age when he hung upon the tree. Had he come solely to manifest God in the flesh, possessing no death-seed, he would have been translated without tasting death, as was Enoch, who walked with God centuries before him. But blessed be his name, he "by the grace of God should taste death for every man" (Heb. 2:9).

In Practice

What Jesus accomplished for us at Calvary must be constantly applied to our life and living. "They that are Christ's have crucified the flesh with its affections and lusts" (Gal. 5:24). Death to self, as well as to sin, is the daily cross we must take up as his followers. Paul could declare himself as one "crucified with Christ," and glorying only in the Cross of our Lord Jesus, "by whom the world is crucified unto me, and I unto the world" (Gal. 2:20; 6:14). Can we confess with the apostle that we bear in every part of our life the Calvary marks of the Lord Jesus (Gal. 6:17)? If we believe in a crucified Savior, it is imperative that we live a crucified life. Isaac Watts has taught us to sing:

> His dying crimson like a robe,
>   Spreads o'er His body on the tree;
> Then I am dead to all the globe,
>   And all the globe is dead to me.

In Paradise

When we come to gaze upon the five bleeding wounds he bears, it will be to discover that—

> The Lamb is all the glory
> Of Emmanuel's land.
> *Anne R. Cousin*

The last book of the Bible makes it abundantly clear that as the slain Lamb, Jesus reigns eternally from the tree. The whole of *The Revelation* revolves around him as "the first begotten of the dead . . . who washed us from our sins in his own blood" (1:5). The Glory Song we are to sing is vibrant with the truth of him who was slain and redeemed us to God by his blood. Even the vast chorus of angels, who have no need of redemption, join in the song, and with a loud voice sing, "Worthy is the Lamb that was slain to receive power, and riches, and wisdom, and strength, and honor, and glory, and blessing" (5:12). When we see the "Lamb as it had been slain," then we'll praise him as we ought. Presently, our hymnbooks are loaded with songs of praise and adoration for all Jesus made possible by his shed blood, and we should make daily use of these to magnify and extol him for all he so willingly endured for us.

> I will sing of my Redeemer,
> And His wondrous love to me;
> On the cruel Cross He suffered,
> From the curse to set me free.
> *James McGranahan*

IN PREACHING

One cannot read the epistles of Paul without realizing how he reveled in the preaching of the Cross. To him, it was the preeminent message to proclaim to a lost world— and what marvelous results were his as he exalted the Son of God who loved him and gave himself for his salvation. Such was the apostle's blessed obsession with this central truth that he determined to know nothing among men, "save Jesus Christ, and him crucified" (1 Cor. 2:2). Without apology he declared, "We preach Christ crucified." Such preaching of the Cross seemed foolish to those perishing in their sins, but to all desiring salvation such a redeeming message was the power of God to save and sanctify (1 Cor. 1:18–25).

Exhorting the Corinthians to keep in memory the gospel he preached unto them, Paul reminded them of its content: "Christ died for our sins according to the scriptures; and that he was buried, and that he rose again the third day according to the scriptures" (1 Cor. 15:3). The spiritual impoverishment of modern preaching can be traced to the bloodless gospel preached. Too many pulpits are silent when it comes to the preaching of the Cross as the only hope for a lost world. How apt is the epigram of Richard Whately of the early nineteenth century, who became the Archbishop of Dublin:

> "Preach not because you have to say something, but because you have something to say."

Preachers have something to say if, with Spirit-inspired lips, they proclaim the message of a crucified Savior who has transformed millions of lives. Further, the preachers who preach the gospel of redeeming love the best are those who live the best.

And I, if I be lifted up from the earth, will draw all men unto me (John 12:32).

1 /

Universal Magnetism

The world has witnessed the rise of many men who, because of inborn personal magnetism, and a commanding personality, were able to inspire multitudes to follow them at all costs. Such a man was Napoleon Bonaparte who became Emperor of France. His personal charm and brilliance were mesmeric. Alas, however, his unique power to draw spellbound men to follow him faded away when he was expelled from the very country he had conquered. But Christ's self-declared magnetism has never diminished. After almost two millennia it is more potent than ever, for daily he draws uncounted numbers all over the world to himself as the crucified Savior. As expressed in Jamieson, Fausset, and Brown's *Commentary on the Whole Bible:*

"Truly, the death of the Cross, in all its significance, revealed in the light, and borne in upon the heart, by the power of the Holy Spirit, possesses an attraction over the wide world—to civilized and savage, learned and illiterate alike—which breaks down all opposition, assimilates all to itself, and forms of the most heterogeneous and discordant materials a kingdom of surpassing glory, whose uniting principle is adoring subjection 'to Him that loved them.' "

As we approach a meditation on our Lord's description of the kind of death he should die, there are two preparatory thoughts in the narration leading up to the appealing verse before us:

First of all, we have the Greek's request, "Sir, we would see Jesus" (John 12:21). What actually prompted this desire is hard to tell. Perhaps it was curiosity which is often the mother of wonder, and which can become the minister of deathless devotion as in the experience of Zacchaeus (Luke 19:3). On the other hand, heart hunger may have compelled the searchers to see Jesus. Grecian art, music, and philosophy supplied no bread for their dissatisfied souls, and thus they found their way to him who came as the Bread of Life and became a foreshadowing of the great gentile world in its participation in the redemption of the Cross.

Secondly, we have Christ's response, "Except a corn of wheat . . . die" (12:24). Here he stresses the necessity of the death he was to die, namely, *life* springing out of *death*. If their love for the beautiful prompted those Greeks to seek the Beautiful One, then they must realize that he cannot be known after the flesh. It is only as the Crucified One that he can be received and admired; the Cross is the only way in which the prince of this world could be defeated and salvation procured for all men, whether Gentiles or Jews. As the corn of wheat, Jesus fell into the ground and died, and what a rich and plentiful harvest has been his. If he was to bless mankind, he must bleed.

HIS MAGNETIC PERSON: "I, if I"

The repeated personal pronoun magnifies his adorable Person. Here we have "The *Christ* of the Cross," for he himself is the most magnetic of all figures and forces. The

I, never offensive when used by Christ, is prominent in his teaching and implies, "I and I alone." This stupendous claim identifies him as the great I AM. With us, the big *I* is repulsive and begets a distasteful egotism, but with him it was so different. Leaving *his* lips, it carried authority and dominion. His words and works were mighty because of who and what he was. Deity is wrapped up in the pronoun and is thus the bridge long enough to span the gulf between sin and God.

The two thieves were lifted up from the earth with Christ, but their blood had no saving efficacy because of who and what they were. The blood shed on the middle Cross was that of the God-Man, the sinless One, the blood of God, as Paul puts it in Acts 20:28. It is because of the divinity of the blood that it offers an efficacious atonement to "a world of sinners lost, and ruined by the Fall." Further, it would seem as if the assertion, "I, and I alone," was used in contrast to the usurpation of Satan, "the prince of darkness," whom Christ unmasked in verse 31. What a study of opposites! The Light of the World—and the prince of darkness! The former draws us to life; the latter, to death: the one draws us to himself with the cords of love; the other draws us by his deceit and crafty subtlety. The Cross provided the death-ray to destroy sin and Satan.

His Magnetic Passion: "Lifted up from the earth"

It is Luke who uses the term *passion* to describe all that Christ endured. "He showed himself alive after his passion" (Acts 1:3). His last week on earth is known as "Passion Week." So we pass from his person to his passion, from his deity to his death, from his character to his Cross, which brings us to think not only of "The Christ of the Cross," but, "The Christ *on* the Cross." It is profitable to note that Jesus used the phrase "lifted up," three times to describe different aspects of Calvary:

The Reason of the Cross: "Even so must the Son of man be lifted up" (John 3:14). In the third chapter of John he is dealing with regeneration, the basis of which is redemption. There can be no salvation without sacrifice.

The Revelation of the Cross: "When ye have lifted up . . . know that I am he" (John 8:28). There were those who wanted to stone him to death because of his revelation of deity, but it is through his being nailed to the Cross, then lifted up upon it, between heaven and earth, that he became a spectacle for the world to see. It was then that he revealed himself as the Son of God when he pardoned the repentant dying thief and gave him the assurance of paradise.

The Reign of the Cross: "Lifted up . . . will draw" (John 12:32). In spite of all the philosophies of men, the Cross is still the great *draw.* The word used here for the phrase "lifted up" suggests an honorable advancement, "If I be exalted." Jesus thought of sufferings as his honor. Although crucifixion was the Roman form of death meted out to malefactors, when he was nailed to the tree he made it his throne from which to reign, not only in the hearts of men, but as Conqueror of the prince of darkness. Thus, in these three verses, the prophecy of Scripture, the ministry of the Spirit, and the perpetual power of the Crucified One are blessedly blended. The R. V. margin has it "lifted out of the earth." He was lifted *up on* the earth at his death, lifted *out* of the earth at his resurrection, and lifted up *from* the earth altogether at his ascension. It takes all that is wrapped up in these three cardinal facts of the Christian faith to complete his drawing power.

HIS MAGNETIC POWER: "I . . . will draw all men after me"

From "The Christ *of* the Cross," and "The Christ *on* the Cross," we come to "The Christ *through* the Cross."

The only way a sinner can reach God is through the Cross, upon which Christ became, not only as the Savior, but as the Mediator between God and men. It has been suggested by a gifted devotional writer that the magnetism of Calvary can be viewed in a threefold way:

"He lifts men up and unites them to God by *revelation,* by the Spirit of *divine light* whereby the reign of *night* is ended—unites them to God by *redemption,* by the gift of *divine life,* whereby the reign of *death* is ended—unites them to God by inspiration, by the gift of *divine liberty,* whereby the reign of *infirmity* is ended."

There are several precious truths we cannot escape as we think of Calvary's compelling power.

1. *The uplifted Lord is the only magnetic power.*

What other truth awakens men to a life of surrender and of devotion like that of the Cross? At Calvary we realize that love so amazing, so divine demands the best we have to give. Paul revelled in the preaching of the Cross because he saw how it thawed the frozen indifference of some hearts, delivering them from a dangerous inertia. He had witnessed how such a message disturbed the conscience, created moral pains, accomplished a spiritual resurrection, and drew the saved to a life of undying love.

Sacrifice is always strangely majestic, and this is why, in common life, it never fails to arouse admiration. Several years ago in an *In Memoriam* column of a daily paper the following notice appeared: "In memory of a lovely little lady, who made the supreme sacrifice of motherhood, leaving sweet memories but a brokenhearted hubby." It was a touching tribute that moved many hearts. Yet somehow the vast majority of people are unresponsive to the supreme sacrifice of all time. A trashy novel can move them to tears, but to their cold, dead hearts, Calvary with all its suffering, horror, and anguish has no appeal. Calvary is nothing to them as they pass by.

For the most effective spiritual results in preaching, everything depends upon how Christ is presented. If he is exalted as an ethical teacher only, such a true aspect may arrest the mind, but it will never generate heat in a frozen heart.

If he is heralded as a fiery reformer, signatures may be gained from those willing to join in a crusade against glaring evils.

If he is presented merely as a fearless young prophet, a cheap, blind worship and mental assent may be secured from those who are out for hero worship.

If, however, he is proclaimed as the sacrificial Savior, and exalted as man's only hope for deliverance from the penalty, power, and pollution of sin, then miracles of transformed lives will happen. As a gifted teacher, ardent reformer, zealous prophet, he may win the plaudits of men, but as the Son of God, crucified for sinners, he captivates their souls and moves them to holier living and consecrated endeavor in his service. An uncounted host are persuaded that their only magnet is the uplifted Lord in the wonderful energies of his transcendent sacrifice, and not in his unmatched teachings and incomparably holy life, even though these added virtue to his efficacious death.

2. *Being lifted up, or above the earth, he can draw from beneath.*

The Christ some men preach can never draw needy hearts to him, for they keep him on the earth. They declare that he was only a man, withal a good man, but no higher than others. Relegating him thus to the level of ordinary humanity, such a perverted Gospel has no magnetism whatever. Had Christ remained on the earth, and died naturally, there would have been no redemption for a lost world. Crucified, however, he conquers. Slain, he can save. A church, or a professed Christian, living on the level of the world can never draw the sinful to the Savior. Like him, they must be raised from the earth to life in the heavenlies, and exalt Jesus by life and lip, if they would by all means save some.

3. *As the uplifted Savior, he possesses a universal magnetism.*

The emphasis in his affirmation is on *"all* men," men out of every nation, station, and condition of life. His announcement as to the form of his death also proclaimed the universality of his redeeming Gospel. Pentecost with its rapid increase of the church proved the powerful virtue and efficacy to draw all kinds of men unto the Savior, for they not only came out from the Jews, gathered at the Feast from every nation under heaven, but from multitudes of Gentiles afar off. As the crucified, risen, and glorified Lord, he was the desire of all nations, and to him must the gathering of the people be (Hag. 2:7).

The question may be asked, "If Christ, by his Cross, can draw all men unto him, why are not *all* men being drawn?" There can be no doubt about the efficacy of what he accomplished to save all men, hence, the universal attractions focused in the sacrificial energy of his death, "the last fragrant syllable of God's utterance of love." But when God created man He endowed him with free will, and with such freedom he can resist the loving overtures of heaven, as what happened in Eden proves. God never forces man to use his will in his favor—he *draws,* but never *drags;* he never worries souls but wins them. Did not Jesus himself have to say, "I would . . . ye would not"? Thus the *drawing* and the *coming* must be united. The Calvary magnet says, "Come," and "draws" as it pleads (Matt. 12:28). What peace is ours, if we can sing:

He drew me, and I followed on,
Charmed to confess the Voice divine.

The blessed hope is that one day we will witness the glorious appearing of the Savior, and as the Magnet draws all the blood-sheltered ones to himself, we will immediately be drawn up to him with greater speed as filings to a magnet.

4. *The magnetism of the Cross is concentric.*

The dynamic of redemption results in a blessed brotherhood. If a pole is placed in the center of a building and people urged to get to it as soon as possible, what would happen? Why, the nearer they found themselves to the pole, the nearer they would be to one another. The Cross, with its centrality communicates its own attraction to every approaching soul, and by a common energy draws all souls together, making them one in the Savior himself. But somehow the church has missed the blood-red Tree in the center and has created centers of her own, and if men do not travel to such, they suffer expulsion.

The tragedy is that Christianity, which is meant to be the expression of brotherly love and union, has become a caricature, the avenue of strife and isolation. Departing from the Cross, religionists quickly separate from each other, for whenever we choose a self-created form, and fight for a self-conceived interpretation of a creed (forgetting to keep our eyes fixed upon the uplifted Lord), we miss the unifying power of the superlative sacrifice of the Cross. We truly believe that a return to the Crucified One himself would quickly heal lamentable divisions within the church, and she would see men coming to her Lord from every quarter.

5. *The magnetism of the Cross is Christocentric.*

No other lips but Christ's could utter such words as this, "Draw all men *unto me*" (John 12:32). Thus he declared his deity and equality with the Father. As the crucified Savior he is the Center and Circumference of all things. It was "in the midst of a throne" that John beheld him. Christ cannot give his glory to another. All must turn to him, "Come unto *me.*" Is there not a modern tendency to bring men to his works, words, and ways, rather than to himself as the Redeemer? Is it not sadly possible to draw people to a church, but not to Christ? But nothing must obscure or misplace him, and our ultimate goal must ever be the bringing of souls to him who alone can bestow eternal life.

> Drawn to the Cross which Thou hast blessed
> With healing gifts for souls distressed
> To find in Thee my life, my rest,
> Christ crucified, I come.
> *Genevieve Mary Irons*

May it always be our passion to present Jesus in all his grace and charm, that hearts will be overwhelmed in contemplation of his majesty. Martyrs like Stephen were forced into death, but Jesus walked deliberately to his bitter end. Willingly he descended the slope of sacrifice until he tore out death's sting, and in one supreme victory he triumphed over sin, death, hell, and Satan. This is why he, and he alone, can deliver men from the prison house of guilt, and from a Christless death with its awful doom of abiding wrath to follow.

> Lifted up was He to die,
> "It is finished!" was His cry;
> Now in Heaven exalted high:
> Hallelujah! What a Saviour!
> *P. P. Bliss*

2 /

Dumb before His Shearers

The fifty-third chapter of Isaiah contains one of the greatest pictures of Calvary ever painted. It is the most impressive record of the sufferings of Christ to appear in the Bible. Every verse supplies us with some glimpse of the Crucified, yet the vision was given to the prophet some 700 years before Christ was born, and before the rise of the Roman Empire when the mode of death by crucifixion was introduced. And there is nothing more helpful to faith than to go to our knees and read this chapter slowly, praying as we read for the Spirit-inspired Calvary vision. Only thus can we enter into the inner meaning of the death of him who was stricken, smitten of God, and afflicted.

Let us look at one precious verse, even at the seventh verse, which Philip found the eunuch reading, and from which he preached Jesus so effectively as to win the noble African for the Savior. It offers two blessed aspects of the vicarious sufferings of Him who was wounded for our transgressions and bruised for our iniquities. For example, we have:

1. The Surrender of Self—"He is brought as a lamb to the slaughter."
2. The Silence of Self—"As a sheep before her shearers is dumb so he openeth not his mouth."

Such divisions indicate two phases of the self-life hard to conquer, namely, self-resistance and self-defense. Reverently, then, may we closely examine this blood-red verse as it came to us from the pen of the Old Testament Calvary prophet.

BROUGHT AS A LAMB—or, The Surrender of Self

The nine words of this first phrase are like a string of precious rubies. They offer us a rich triad of truth regarding the Death of our Lord.

1. *His death was voluntary*—"He was brought" (or "led"). Jesus was not forced or dragged to his Cross. He was not taken there against his will, or compelled to go by stronger power. He was led! He was oppressed and afflicted! And such language implies the voluntary acceptance of the Cross. "He let himself be afflicted." What amazing grace! His life was not taken: it was given. He had the power to lay down his life and take it up again: and he did both. O truth sublime! Jesus was not driven to Calvary. He was drawn to it by love to God—and by his passion to save a world of sinners lost and ruined by the fall.

2. *His death was vicarious*—"As a lamb." Doubtless the prophet had in mind the Paschal Lamb, offered up instead of the sinful Israelite, when as he laid his hand upon the head of the unblemished lamb, a double transfer took place. First, the forgiveness of God was assured through the holy lamb, offered and slain. Then the sin of the offerer was removed as he confessed his guilt over the head of the victim. The knife Abraham meant to plunge into the heart of Isaac

ultimately slew the ram caught in the thicket. The ram died for Isaac, and God's Ram died for me. Is it not somewhat strange that this phrase forms the central part of the chapter? Surely it is the central truth of the gospel! We are redeemed by the precious blood of God's Holy Lamb.

The blood of beasts could not give a guilty conscience peace, nor wash away its stain, but as Isaac Watts goes on to sing:

> But Christ the heavenly Lamb,
> Takes all our sins away;
> A sacrifice of nobler name
> And richer blood, than they.

3. *His death was vicious*—"To the slaughter." Slaughter! It is a cruel word, suggesting the brutality of the death of God's innocent, holy Lamb. Every lamb slain in Israel's day died in a humane way affording the least pain to the innocent animal. But who can measure the shame, indignities, and brutal assaults heaped upon God's Lamb? There was no consideration for his feelings. No wonder nature surrounded the Cross with a robe of darkness thus covering up the viciousness of men as seen in the mangled form of the world's Redeemer!

SILENT AS A SHEEP—or, The Silence of Self

The last part of this verse describes the greatest piece of heroism ever witnessed by the eyes of men. The suffering of innocence is ever nobler than the deserved suffering of guilt. Because of who and what he was, the pang of suffering penetrated the heart of Jesus, yet he held his peace. We further glean three truths regarding his work on behalf of unworthy sinners.

1. *His Identification*—"As a Sheep." Jesus is often called "The Shepherd," but this is the only time he is called a

"sheep." And he is both, just as he is priest and sacrifice—God and man. Doubtless there is some connection with the "sheep" of verse 6: the straying sheep. Being made in the likeness of sinful flesh, he appears to die as a sheep. At his baptism he identified himself with our fallen race, and the climax of this identification was at the Cross, where in some mysterious way he gathered up our sin and made it his own. He was made sin for us! He was numbered with the transgressors! Isaiah tells us that Jesus made his grave with the wicked, and with the rich in his death, or "deaths," as the margin quotes it. Deaths! Yes, he died the deaths of all! He tasted death for every man. What a bitter draught it must have been!

2. *His Humiliation*—"Before her shearers is dumb." It is an affecting scene to watch a sheep shorn of its beautiful wool. I always feel a cold shudder passing over me as I watch a newly shorn sheep skipping over the field. And as shearers have one aim, namely that of stripping the sheep of its natural covering, may we not detect in the figure as used by Isaiah a reference to the deep humiliation of the Savior? Jesus came before his shearers who stripped him of his wool, gambling for the possession of such. "They part my garments among them, and cast lots upon my vesture" (Ps. 22:18). His foes might have had the decency to leave him his clothes, but no. He died naked and exposed to the cold, as well as to shame. Yes, and his nakedness was a type of the sinner's wretchedness, who "naked, come to him for dress." Sheep give their wool that others might be covered. The garments we presently wear represent the surrender a multitude of sheep were forced to make. And so the humiliation, shame, and stripping of the Savior provide the warm, eternal robe of righteousness and salvation for all mankind.

3. *His Self-Abnegation*—"He openeth not his mouth." This brings us to the glorious victory of Christ over his

anguish and shame. If you watch a sheep being shorn or slain you will find that it submits most silently. Three times over Isaiah tells us that Jesus was silent. Twice we read, "He openeth not his mouth." Once, that he was "dumb." And such fits in with the three occasions the Savior was silent when facing his enemies.

Before the Jewish Rulers, Jesus held his peace.

Facing Pilate, he answered nothing.

And standing before Herod, he answered him nothing.

He could have loudly protested his innocence. One breath from him would have slain all those who clamored for his blood, even as they were stricken to the ground upon the sight of him at Gethsemane. But by his attitude our blessed Lord not only manifested the surrender of self in that he allowed cruel men to lead him out to his death: but also the silence of self in that he never uttered one word in his defense, although he knew he was hated without a cause.

And why did he suffer in silence? Because he knew that Calvary was the will of God for him. Although his death was not deserved, it was decreed. It pleased the Lord to bruise him! The Psalmist answers this mystery in the words: "I was dumb, I opened not my mouth; because thou didst it" (Ps. 39:9). What death to self-defense! Here, then, are two avenues of victory if we care to follow our smitten, silent Lord. We must be willing to be:

1. *Led as lambs.* A lamb is a young sheep, and because Jesus died at the early age of thirty-three, he claims all the powers of youth. A lamb is frisky, the emblem of innocency, activity, and freshness. May God give us grace to lead our lambs to the altar, even as Abraham led Isaac!

There is another application, however, of this phrase. Often we render a good deal of forced work in our service for the Lord. Since we act under compulsion, our religious life and work is a treadmill existence. We lack the lamblike character of submission, willing surrender, as well as purity.

Shrinking from the slaughter, we try to save our selves! We are not willing to be "accounted as sheep for the slaughter," as Paul puts it in Romans 8:36. O for grace to die to our own will and way, and to be led as lambs!

2. *Silent as sheep*. Peter tells us that in his silence Jesus left us an example to follow. Although reviled, he reviled not again: and when he suffered he threatened not. But do we follow his steps in such silent submission? How do we act when we come before our shearers? Are we silent or assertive—dumb or defensive? When shorn of our reputation, position, place or office, how do we act? Do we immediately raise our voices in our own defense, stoutly contending for our rights? The Calvary way is—SILENCE! "But, O Lord, it is a hard and difficult road for our feet to travel! We like to protest our innocence." And the only answer to our cry is that, he was innocent; he did not deserve to die. His death was the greatest blunder ever made, yet he allowed it, passing out to the cruel, unjust judgment and bitterness of the Cross—SILENT! We love to fight, argue, and claim our rights, and show people that we are not to be sat on— *Jesus held his peace.*

Yes, and when it comes to the slaughter of our ambitions, and to the shearing of many dear things in life, it may be hard to accept such as part of God's will. Yet as we walk the blood-red way, it is wonderful to see him justifying our surrender and silence. And how many there are who are dumb, opening not their mouths against the mysterious dealings of God! All honor to these silent sufferers! Have you met many of them on life's journey? Mothers, heavily laden with the cares of home, yet never murmuring. Pain-stricken, diseased, and lonely souls who never complain or rebel. Noble hearts, who, although misjudged and treated adversely, suffer in silence, drinking deeply of the spirit of the Silent Sufferer of Calvary. May we all be found in such august company!

Read Psalm 22.

3 /

Photograph of Our Lord's Saddest Hours

It was C. H. Spurgeon, the renowned Baptist preacher, who wrote of Psalm 22 —

"It is the photograph of our Lord's saddest hours;
It is the record of His dying words;
It is the bottle of His last tears;
It is the memorial of His expiring joys"—and we can add;
It is the declaration of his glorious conquest.

There are three Psalms related to "the sufferings of Christ, and the glory that should follow" (2 Cor. 1:5). They form a blessed trilogy, namely—

Psalm 22. The Psalm of the Cross, the Sword, and the Substitute. Here we see Jesus as the *Good Shepherd* dying on earth (John 10:11).

Psalm 23. The Psalm of the Crook, the Staff, and the Shepherd. Here we see Jesus as the *Great Shepherd,* risen and in heaven (Heb. 13:20).

Psalm 24. The Psalm of the Crown, the Scepter, and the Sovereign. Here we see Jesus as the *Chief Shepherd,* coming in His glory to earth again (1 Peter 5:4).

We have Mount Calvary on one side, Mount Zion on the other, and the Valley of the Shadow of Death in between. Although Psalm 22 is referred to in its title as "A Psalm of David," a greater than David is here. It is the most marvelous of all the Psalms, one that Jesus made his own on the Cross, and one that drips with his ruby-blood of redemption. As our eyes are opened by the Holy Spirit we see here no man, save Jesus only. Here, hundreds of years before the Cross, is mirrored the innermost workings of the Savior's heart in the crisis of conflict.

The prophecy of this Psalm assumes the vividness and literalness of actual history. What is prophecy but history— written in advance? Jesus is in every syllable of this Psalm, and this is why in his hour of desolation he made it his own as he came to die. Ancient traditions say that he recited the whole Psalm, beginning as it does with the fourth cry of the Cross, and ending with the seventh cry, "It is finished," which is the original of "he hath done this" (Ps. 22:31). No matter what reflection of David's own trials and triumphs may suggest, the Psalmist is an eminent type of the Messiah. Thus, as face answers to face in a glass, so this inspired prophecy became actual history at Calvary. It prefigures the two great divisions of Christ's mediatorial career, namely, his humiliation and his exaltation.

Taking the Psalm as a whole we find ourselves gazing down into the depths of woe, then upwards and onwards to the heights of glory. Doubtless David himself experienced many of the sorrows he describes, for he knew the fear of the deepest depths of adversity and soul-travail, and also the heights of prosperity and raptures of heavenly joy. But his own acquaintance, sorrowful and joyful, was intensified and transfigured until he became a unique type of the incarnate Savior. In his Psalms, David, by the Spirit, became the prophet, inspired to portray the emotions of his Greater Son a thousand years later. Who but the omniscient Spirit could reveal to a human mind so far in advance the inner workings in the heart of Christ? This mirror of the crucifixion is all the more remarkable when we remember that this Roman form of capital punishment did not come into existence until the Empire was founded centuries later.

ITS DESIGNATION

It is thought by some that the Hebrew inscription, *Aijeleth Shahar,* was the name of a musical instrument accompanying the singing of the Psalm. The English translation of the title of this heart-moving ode is suggestive, *Hind of the Morning.* The hind is renowned for its comeliness, loveliness, and grace, as it leaps over mountains and skips over hills. Because of its beauty and value it is pursued by hunters, set at bay and surrounded and harassed to death by dogs. As the hind faced the goring of bulls, the roaring of lions, and the worry of dogs, all encompassing the animal waiting to tear its flesh asunder, it provides a fitting emblem of God's Hind who was ever hunted from the moment of his birth, with Herod's edict of the death of all male children, right on until the Pharisees gloated over his cruel end. It is said that the timidity of the hind is ascribed to its large heart in which there is a bone shaped like a cross: and that its hot breath entices serpents out of their lair to death. This we know, the hot, fevered, dying breath of Jesus meant victory over that old serpent, the devil.

But it is the hind of the *morning* which envisages the dawn of brighter and better days. Thus the title finally compacts the theme of the Psalm, namely that of a black night of affliction opening to morn, and the hastening to a noontide of joy and gladness. The first rays of the morning sun have been likened to the horns of a hind. As we approach the construction of the Psalm we feel something of the awe Moses felt at the bush. We feel that we should take off our shoes for the place whereon we stand is holy ground.

ITS DIVISION

It would appear that two main parts constitute the Psalm as a whole. These became Christ's prayer and plea on the Cross—humiliation and exaltation: suffering and glory: travail and triumph. See 1 Peter 1: 11. But examining it closely we discern the following divisions:

1. *Crucifixion,* verses 1–21a—Redemption, Travail, Sufferings as Priest.

2. *Conquest,* verses 21b–26—Resurrection, Triumph, Offices as Prophet.

3. *Crown,* verses 27–31—Crown, Reign, Throne, Offices as King.

TRAVAIL (1–21a)

1. The Anguish of Spirit (22:1–5)

In this first section the sufferings of Jesus are copiously described, and we are given a minute unveiling of Calvary with its blackness, tempest of woe, torture, and ignominy. The alternatives of sorrow and complaint, and urgent appeal are easily traceable in these opening verses. Here we have the laying bare of anguish in the innermost soul, and the upward look and cry for help. The Psalm was a balm for the Savior's pierced heart. As such it is precious to all who drink his cup. The threefold complaint answers to the scriptural recognition of the threefold division of our humanity, desolation of divine abandonment to ransom us from the same dreadful woe. Although he cried in the daytime and nighttime, the complaint was, *Thou hearest not.* Formerly, he could say of the Father, "Thou hearest me always," but now, in his dire need, the heavens seemed as brass.

Yet with all his surprise, perplexity, and bewilderment, he could still say, *"My God!"* an appellation occurring four times in the Psalm. He is still *his* God, although hidden. He was as tender as ever, but Jesus had not the human consciousness and sensible enjoyment of his presence. The reason for this anguish of spirit was his willingness to bear our curse, and to become the Sin-bearer, and to provide consolation for all deserted lives.

> But none of the ransomed ever knew
> How deep were the waters crossed;
> Nor how dark was the night the Lord passed through,
> Ere He found His sheep that was lost.
> *Elizabeth C. Clephane*

1. THE APPEAL (3–5)

How could such desertion be reconciled to the holy character of God? Yet, in spite of the seeming contradiction there was a reason for this seeming desolation. Although God's ear was closed, his helping hand withheld, and his countenance hidden, yet there was no mistrust ripening into despair. If faith's vision is shrouded in darkness, the hand of faith clings with a desperate grasp. "*But* thou art holy." The reason for the closed eyes and heart is given by the prophet "Thou canst not look on iniquity" (Heb. 1:13). At the dread moment of his cry, Jesus was bearing the terrible load of the sin of the world. If it seemed as if God was not answering the prayer of his Son, his character is ever the same, and he can never act contrary to his nature. Three times over in this appeal the word *trusted* appears. If this is true of us will our children base their plea to God upon our devotion to him? Faith always justifies God, although we may not be able to grasp the significance of divine dealings at the time. Faith still trusts when it cannot trace. *Thou hearest not.* God's silence is no reason for ours. It should be an incentive to greater importunity (Matt. 15:22–25).

2. The Anguish of Soul (22:6–11)

This portion carries two aspects:
The cause of human reproach and reviling (6–8)
The appeal appended to the complaint (9–11).

THE COMPLAINT (6–8)

In these verses the Son turns from his Father in heaven to mockery of men on the earth—from his inner consciousness to the outer estate. First, we have the sorest agony wrapping the innermost spirit in the horrors of great darkness, so hard to endure in One so pure and tender and gracious. But the second grief was very keen and cutting, namely, the treatment of sinful men. Jesus was despised and rejected of men, and in effect he prays, "O God, the fathers of old were the objects of thy care and relief, why not *me,* thy Son?" We have the taunt flung at him as he died upon the Cross, "He trusted in God: let him deliver him now" (Matt. 27:43).

In this Psalm we meet one of the most forceful *buts* of Scripture, "*But* I am a worm, and no man; a reproach of men, and despised of the people" (22:6). Although Jesus came as the great I AM, being made a little lower than the angels, he now regards himself as a worm, comparable to a helpless, powerless, downtrodden worm, and passive in being crushed. He seemed to be devoid of any might except the strength to suffer. The word used for *worm* here is not an ordinary word, but the crimson coccus from which the scarlet dye is extracted—suggestive of the blood that flowed from his riven side. Yet worm though he was in the sight of those who reviled and rejected, he became the worm God was able to use to thrash the mountains.

The laughing scorn and protrusion of lips, deemed in the East as a very strong indication of contempt, imply that he was jeered for having rolled himself upon God without effect (22:6–8)—a forecast of those who mocked him while on the Cross (Matt. 27:39–43). The sufferer, however, turned the taunt into a prayer. Out of derision, deliverance came.

The Appeal (9–11)

Although, at times, trouble seems nearer than God, faith sees the deliverer, and so we have another *But,* "But thou art he." Here in prophecy Christ reminds the Father of the beginning of his incarnate life, and of all that he was to him through childhood, youth, and manhood. Then did he forsake him now—a man after his own heart? Thus we have the plea for the continuance of his Heavenly Father's protection and care, manifested when he was a helpless babe. What he did for him in his feebleness should have been the pledge that he would protect him now that he is being reproached and insulted by his enemies. When we are made to drink of the cup of ridicule, let us consider him who endured such contradiction against ourselves (Heb. 12:3). "Be not far from me" (Ps. 22:11). Amid the trials of life it may seem as if God is hiding his face, but such a feeling is only to the eye of sense; for has he not promised, "Certainly I will be with thee" (Exod. 3:12)?

3. *The Anguish of Body* (22:12–21)

This section seems to fall into two parts—the more outward torture and shame of the Cross, with a literal description of the process of crucifixion with its agony and gradual exhaustion. We are also given emblems of the hatred of men from which God rescued his Son. So we have, first of all, *anguish of spirit* under divine desertion and groans—then *anguish of soul* from human mockery and reviling—

now *anguish of body* related to the actual excruciating pains of such a death. *In verses 12–18* we have the cruel Pharisees, Sadducees and scribes likened unto bulls, lions, and dogs because of their brutality. Not what is noble in these beasts is cited, but the worst to depict what was brutal and devilish. The selection of the animals named symbolizes the hatred of men toward Jesus. By their climax of wickedness they put themselves in alliance with the worst nature of these brutes.

What a vivid photograph of the Cross we are given— the gaping crowds and their abuse, bones wrenched one from another, the broken heart, fevered lips, pierced limbs, parted garments, the thrusting of Jehovah's sword against his fellow! But we must not forget the invisible hand overruling and controlling the cruel hands of earth which were the visible instruments causing the death of Jesus.

Then we have the *Appeal,* the last cry for help, and the prelude to rest (19–31). This is the appeal of One clinging intently to a refuge and hope: "Be not far off"; "Thou hast heard me"; "Deliver my darling"; all speak of an urgent and persistent cry for relief. *My darling* suggests my soul, the most precious gem in the casket of the body—my only one, my most valued possession. As it is God's prerogative to hear and answer prayer, this section closes with a prelude of the coming rest of Glory.

TRIUMPH (21–26)

We now pass from the vivid and graphic portrayal of Christ's suffering with its isolation, treading the winepress alone, to the triumph that followed. From the loneliness of his struggle he emerges not into a personal recompense merely but as the Forerunner of vast numbers no man can number. At last the clouds have rolled away, and the black night of affliction and woe open into morning, hence the exclamation of praise.

Commencing the Psalm we are struck with the sudden abruptness of its starting point. Travail of soul comes on us all at once, then we have the swift response of effectual help, and we leap from storm to calm, from darkness to day. Such a sudden transition must have taken place in the soul of Jesus, as amid depths of anguish he had gleams of glory. Is this not also true in the life of many a saint, experiencing a radiance lighting up the inner chamber, although there are darkness and tempest all around? See Micah 3:6, 8.

Conquest followed the crucifixion, resurrection, and ascension of Jesus. Thus, the forecast of his ministry: "I will declare thy name unto my brethren" (Ps. 22:22), must be linked to Hebrews 2:12, "I will declare thy name unto my brethren," and to John 17:26 and 20:17. Here we see him as the risen, glorified Lord in a tender and intimate relationship with his redeemed ones, his church. "My praise shall be of thee" (Ps. 22:25). Praise originates in him and centers in his redemption. He trod the winepress alone. None were with him to divide his woe, but now all can share his triumph, and mutual kinship as his brethren, branches, bride and bone of his bone. Such a blessed relationship is the privileged issue of all his travail.

The meek eat and are satisfied. In instituting his Supper, our Lord spoke of eating his flesh which meant the appropriation by faith of all he accomplished, and of all he is in himself. There is no food, no peace of heart, no strength for obedience in a Christ who did not die as the Substitute for sinners. As the Sacrifice offered to God, he is our peace and sustenance, and we are fully satisfied as we feed upon him who became our bruised and broken Bread.

THRONE (27–31)

What a ring of royal dominion about this last portion of the Calvary Psalm! Though he was crucified as a rejected

King, the kingdom is now his, and he reigns where the sun doth his successive journeys run. Not only his brethren, the Jews, but all the ends of the world, the Gentiles, are to turn to and worship him. With universal dominion Jesus will see of the travail of his soul and be satisfied. The usurper is dethroned, and the universality of his victory is recognized by the comprehensiveness of the welcome afforded him. Peoples from later generations will bend their knees before him, as he rules among the nations. Poet Hopps has taught us to sing:

> Tyrant thrones and idol shrines,
>   Let them from their place be hurled;
> Enter on Thy better reign,
>   Wear the crown of this poor world.

Jesus may not be recognized as governor by the nations today, but his day is coming when, because he became the slain Lamb, he will be seen as the Lion. The scars of Calvary will bring his sovereignty and the Cross his crown. "He hath done this," or "It is finished," and his reign from shore to shore will bring the consummation of his work.

Jesus Christ, and him crucified.
. . . words . . . which the Holy
Spirit teacheth (1 Cor. 2:2, 13).

4 /

The Cross As a Divine Revelation

The Bible is not a riddle to resolve but a revelation to receive and believe, and it is only as we believe that the Holy Spirit is its Divine Author, that we can prove it to be a divine revelation. Doubt this declared fact, and the Bible will close its treasure chest and refuse to display its gems. But give it faith, trust, obedience, and love, then we possess an untold mine of wealth.

The Bible is not a production of man's thoughts as all other books are, whether religious or otherwise, but a revelation of divine thought in human language. Therefore as its Author was a witness of the One who was hanged to a tree (Acts 5:33), his unfolding of the Cross throughout Scripture is authentic. There are three indisputable facts about the Word we must not forget:

1. *It is a revelation from God*

As such it is *authoritative,* and as the law of the Lord, it bears his seal. The constant refrain, "Thus saith the Lord," is the stamp of divine authority. Then it is *infallible,* inerrant, and absolute. The law of the Lord is perfect, otherwise it would never be able to convert a soul. In its original form, it contained no mistakes, an evidence of divine inspiration. It is also a *final* revelation. While it contains a progressive revelation of God and his purpose, it is now a final unfolding, with nothing to add or delete. Certainly, fresh truth flashes from its sacred pages, but these truths are always, "*out* of thy law."

2. *It is a revelation by God*

As he is its Giver, he is the best interpreter of it. As the revelation from, and by, God to man, it unfolds all he needs both here and hereafter. Further, its truth is not discerned by the light of natural reason, but can only be spiritually discerned by the Holy Spirit who inspired holy men of old to express it in human language (1 Cor. 2:14). With the Spirit as our constant Teacher, we can understand the assertion of John, "Ye need not that any man teach you" (1 John 2:27). But we bless God for Spirit-taught teachers.

3. *It is a revelation about God*

The central figure of the Bible is God manifest in flesh. The Living Word and The Written Word are wedded together. Christ as God is seen set in the sky of Scripture, and the great and grand object of such a sublime revelation is to lead us to apprehend, appreciate, and appropriate Christ as the Word made flesh for our salvation. As we have already indicated, the key of the Bible is Christ and his Cross. He is the central Person, and his Cross, the central theme. The two phrases, "There they crucified him" and "It is finished" (John 19:18, 30), form the inner heart of the Bible. The heart of Christianity is the Bible, the heart of the Bible, the Cross, and the heart of the Cross, the very heart of God himself, who is the Source of sacrificial love. "Herein is love, not that we loved God, but that he loved us"; "God so loved the world that he gave his only begotten Son" (1 John 4:10; John 3:16).

The threefold proof that redemption was Christ's finished work is revealed in no uncertain terms: *In his resurrection.* "I . . . was dead . . . I am alive for evermore" (Rev. 1:18). There can be no further demand because the debt was paid, once for all. "Himself purged our sins." *In his ascension.* Redemption accomplished, he ascended into heaven and "sat down on the right hand of the Majesty on high" (Heb. 1:3). Sitting down implied a completed task. *In our regeneration.* In his conversation with Nicodemus, Jesus declared that without redemption there cannot be regeneration; that the new birth is the fruit of his death. "Even so must the Son of man be lifted up" (John 3:14). On the basis of such sacrifice, "Ye must be born again" (John 3:7). In conviction, the Holy Spirit works on the basis of the Cross and applies the truth to the believing sinner.

The centrality of the Cross, then, is the prominent theme of revelation. It is the center to which our minds are directed. We see it as:

Central in the eternal purpose of God. The Cross was not an afterthought, suddenly produced to meet an emergency, for Jesus came as the Lamb slain *before* the foundation of the world. Calvary was deliberately planned in the dateless past.

Central in the revelation of God. All planets of truth revolve around this sun. The Cross stands related to all other themes, and it is the assurance of the fulfillment of all divine promises.

Central at Calvary. Christ's position in the midst was not coincidental, but divinely arranged, for the Cross ever divides, as the opposite reactions of the two thieves who died with Jesus indicate. He is either the savor of life, or the savor of death.

Central in glory. John, in "The Revelation," proclaims that the slain Lamb is adored above. "The Lamb is all the glory in Immanuel's land." As the Lamb, he is in the midst of the throne.

Central in the believer's life of victory. Paul stressed the necessity of a crucified life as an evidence of faith in a crucified Savior. "I am crucified with Christ" (Gal. 2:20). Ours is not a self-crucifixion, but the constant application, by the Holy Spirit, of Christ's death to daily life and living— a daily reckoning of ourselves as being dead to all that is alien to the word and will of God. This was the message, central in Paul's ministry.

Further, in the complete Revelation God has provided in Scripture, the Cross appears as a prism with a sevenfold ray which the church should never forget:

1. *The Wondrous Love of God* (John 3:16)

Because God *is* Love, he drew salvation's plan. Although the One sinned against, he was the One who provided the remedy for all who have sinned against him. He condemned the sinner and gave his Son to bear the curse and its punishment. Thus the Cross was not the cause but the effect of divine love. What a striking statement regarding the loving purpose of God Peter gave in his Christ-exalting sermon: "Him, being delivered by the determinate counsel and foreknowledge of God" (Acts 2:23).

2. *Liberty and Joy* (Rom. 5:10, 11)

Another blessed result of our reception of the Atonement is a present, perpetual salvation by the glorified life of Jesus. Being reconciled (or being saved by the *death* of Christ), we shall be saved by his *life.* And not only so, but we also joy in God through our Lord Jesus Christ, by whom we have received the atonement, or reconciliation. We "Joy in God," not in ourselves, because of a daily deliverance from the power, government, and allurements of sin through him who is alive forevermore.

3. *Complete Ownership* (1 Cor. 6:19, 20)

By his lacerated body, Jesus paid the price to purchase all we are and have; and we are to bear in our body the Calvary marks. "Your body is the temple of the Holy Spirit. . . . Ye are bought with a price therefore glorify God in your body, and in your spirit which are God's" (1 Cor. 6:19, 20). The human temple is to be filled with the glory of him who died to make us his very own.

4. *Provisions for All Our Needs* (Rom. 8:32)

As the greater includes the lesser, having given his most precious possession, his only begotten Son, he can now bestow upon us all necessary things whether natural, physical, or spiritual. Note that the free bestowal comes *with him.* Apart from Christ as *the* Gift of God, we have no gifts.

5. *Emancipation from the Lamb* (Col. 2:14–23)

Twin truths are here emphasized by Paul, namely, liberty from the condemnation of the law, which Jesus nailed to his Cross; and victory over Satan and satanic forces. By his death he spoiled these principalities and powers, triumphing over them. We sing about "marching on *to* victory." But should it not be "marching on *from* victory," even the victory of the Cross? As Satan is a defeated foe, faith can appropriate the conquest already secured. Freedom from the law does not mean license, but is an imperative reason for obedience. We are to become inlawed to Christ.

6. *Incentive to Holiness and Preparation* (Titus 2:11–13)

In this great passage we have evidence of how the Cross is wedded to other truths. Because Christ gave himself for our salvation from the penalty and guilt of sin, and, by his Spirit, purifies us as a people for his own possession, we are to look for his promised return as our *great God.* If ours is the blessed hope of his glorious appearing, then we cannot live just any kind of a life. We must be more holy.

7. *Basis of Christ's Love-work for His Church* (Eph. 5:25–27)

What a sublime revelation Paul packs into these three verses, in which he links the Cross to marital relationships! Three aspects of the Savior's work are discernible in this great passage:

His Past Work: "Christ also loved the church, and gave himself for it" (Eph 5:25). With his own blood he bought her to be his bride.

His Present Work: "That he might sanctify and cleanse it." Made clean by his blood, we are kept clean by his Word.

His Prospective Work: "To present it to himself a glorious church." When he presents us faultless to the Father, then Jesus will see of the travail of his soul, and be eternally satisfied.

5 /

Love That Stoops

The whole of the verse before us is captured as C. H. Scofield expresses it: "The Christian life is the outliving of the inliving Christ." It has, therefore, a most important bearing upon our Christian life in its entirety. The verse seems to contain seven spiritual wonders, and although it is not our intention to expound all seven, (but only one), yet we can glance at them in passing.

1. That Christ should love and die for a sinner like Paul. Referring to his past life out of Christ, he said, "Who loved me, and gave himself for me" (Gal. 2:20).

2. That Christ should be crucified for a *sinner.* As he died for sinners, Paul saw himself "crucified with Christ" (Gal. 2:20).

3. That Christ should give himself, voluntarily, to be crucified, who "gave himself."

4. That Paul should be crucified in Christ. To the apostle it was a co-crucifixion.

5. That Paul should live although crucified. "Nevertheless, I live" (Gal. 2:20) Dead, he was yet alive.

6. That Paul as a crucified man should be indwelt by a

once crucified, but now living Lord. "Christ liveth in me" (Gal. 2:20).

7. That Paul maintains this new life by faith in Christ. Yet not by his own faith alone, but "by the faith of the Son of God" (Gal. 2:20).

He lived by a faith which had as its object the One who had died for him. It is the last phrase of this wondrous verse, magnifying the love and sacrifice of Jesus, that we are now to concentrate upon.

WHO HE IS: *The Son of God*

This title speaks of divine power, position, and authority as God's Representative, and is associated with great crises as the following verses prove (Matt. 4:3; 27:40; Luke 4:41; Rom. 1:4; 1 John 3:8). We are given three glimpses of who this majestic One is.

1. *The Lord of Glory* (1 Cor. 2:8). Had those who rejected him known that "he was the image of the invisible God," and "the first born of every creature," they would not have crucified him. But their eyes were blinded as to his true identity. He was equal with the Father, with supreme power and authority over the hosts of heaven.

2. *The Creator of All.* "He made the worlds" (Heb. 1:2). Christ was the Medium through whom everything around, above, and beneath the earth was brought into being (Col. 1:16). This marvelous Person, who came to die as a Substitute for sinners, was the Light, lighting every man coming into the world (John 1:3, 9).

3. *The Sustainer of Life* (Col. 1:17). Not only was Christ "before all things," but "by him all things consist," or hold together. He was not the pure Jew, fanatic or deluded enthusiast some had pictured him to be, but the One conspicuous for his supreme majesty, power, and dominion. Although he died in extreme weakness as a man, it is all he is in

himself that gave virtue to his death as the Savior. Had he been a mere man, his death would have had no power to redeem.

WHAT HE HAS DONE: *"He loved me, and gave himself for me."*

There are those who appear to love, but never give, and others who give but never love. Christ displayed his love in the act of sacrifice.

Think of his love!

When we think of all his glory and greatness, it would seem as if he was too high and majestic to stoop to love sinners. We are not told that he loved the host in glory over which he was Lord, or the creation he formed for our sake, but that he showered his love upon sinful, rebellious, and disappointing men. What boundless love!

1. *It is unsought.* The marvel is that the initiative was his. While we were yet sinners, he commended his love to us (Rom. 5:8). Herein is love at its highest level, not that we loved him, but his was the first advance (1 John 4:10). The Apostle of Love must have been overwhelmed when he wrote, "He first loved us" (1 John 4:19). The offended, spurned One was the first to manifest love, even for his enemies. We can never win or merit such love, which loves in spite of demerit. Love is not only one of the transcendent virtues of God, but a part of his being: "God *is* love." And he loves the unlovely and the unloveable.

2. *It is undeserved.* How unworthy and undeserving we are of such matchless love, outraged in Eden, trampled upon through the ages, and spurned by multitudes today! Yet like a hound this divine love tracks us down, and seeks, in spite of our sin and rebellion, to woo us back to himself. No wonder John Bunyan exclaimed, "O, Thou loving One, Thou blessed One, Thou deservest to have me. Thou hast

bought me. Thou deservest to have me all. Thou hast paid for me ten thousand times more than I am worth."

3. *It is perfect.* Human love, no matter how intense, has its defects, but the love of God is like himself, perfect as well as pure. It is a love so wonderful, passing the love of the most devoted woman. A woman's love is as tenacious as it is tender. It clings to the one she loves, even though bitter disappointment may be hers. The question is asked, "Can a woman forget the child she bore?" She may, but there is no flaw in divine love. Many waters cannot quench it. It suffers long and is kind. It is a love that will not let us go. Jesus himself said, "Greater love hath no man than this, that a man lay down his life for his friends" (John 15:13). But his love is even greater than this for when we were enemies Jesus loved us and died for our salvation. "There is no love like the love of Jesus never to fade or fall."

4. *It is eternal.* God's message to his sinning people was, "Yea, I have loved thee with an everlasting love" (Jer. 31:3). Jesus assured his disciples that having loved them, he would "love them unto the end" (John 13:1). His love was not born, and it cannot die. It entwines itself within our hearts now, and follows us on over the grave into eternity. No one and nothing, not even death, can separate us from such love (Rom. 8:35–39).

5. *It is personal.* The wonder of God's love is that he set it upon me (Ps. 91:14). Are we not told that Jesus loved Mary, Martha, and Lazarus (John 11:5)? The blessed feature of his love is its personalization, as Paul experienced when he wrote, "The Son of God who loved *me,* and gave himself for *me"* (Gal. 2:20). The apostle was loved of the Lord, even when he was Saul the blasphemer, unbeliever, and persecutor. The sun may shine upon the vast world, yet we can draw the blinds and shut out all its light and glory waiting to flood our little house. Is this not so with God's

eternal love? Oh, that multitudes more would open the shutters of their lives and allow this transforming love to flood their souls! Open ye the doors, and the King of Glory shall come in.

Think of His Gift!

Loving and giving are always united. They are inseparable twins. Sacrifice is the highest evidence of love. Thus Jesus not only loved but gave the best he had, his holy self, for our redemption. Two givings are to be distinguished, namely, the Father's and the Son's. The Father freely gave up his son to death for us all (John 3:16; 1 John 4:9). The Son voluntarily surrendered his life for our salvation (Gal. 2:24). *Giving* has a twofold implication. First of all, it means to yield or surrender, and this was the Godward aspect of redemption. Then it implies to hand over to another, which was what Jesus did when he acquiesced in the will of his Father, and handed over his life as a Substitute for others.

1. *The Gift was Substitutional:* The preposition Paul uses means, on behalf of, or instead of, or in the place of. "Gave himself instead of me." Peter, as well as Paul, loved to present Christ as the sinner's Substitute (1 Peter 2:21; 3:18; 4:11). Dealing with his suffering of death, the writer of *Hebrews* declares that by the grace of God, Jesus tasted death for every man (2:9). The original has the plural for death—*deaths.* It is beyond our finite minds to comprehend this marvelous truth that all deaths were rolled into one death, and that by so dying, death he slew. The blood he shed was that of God's Son, not Mary's Son (1 John 1:7). Deity gives efficacy to his death on our behalf. C. H. Spurgeon was wont to say that his theology could be compressed into four words: *He died for me!*

2. *The Gift was Personal:* Instead of "me," insert your own name, and make the verse your own. *All* have sinned,

and *all* can lay claim to all the Savior provided. Each man's sin caused him to sink beneath the awful load, yet such is the manner of his love that each can become a son of God (1 John 3:1). The verse we have considered begins with *the Son of God* and ends with *me.* What extreme contrasts the same presents, and nothing but his Cross can bring us together and make us one.

> "My need and Thy great fullness meet,
> And I have all in Thee."
>> *H. C. G. Moule*

My God, my God, why hast thou
forsaken me? (Matt. 27:46).

6 /

God Forsaken of God

It was Martin Luther who said that this fourth cry of
the Cross suggested: "God forsaken of God." All that is
associated with this heart-rending cry is too deep and mysterious for a complete explanation. We can only think of the
solemn words with hushed hearts, for here we behold the
Savior in the depth of his sorrows, and in the black midnight
of his anguish. At this moment physical weakness united
with acute mental torture arising from much of the shame
and ignominy through which Jesus passed. As we have seen,
the Psalm foretelling the agonies of Calvary commences
with this poignant cry (22:1). What nine words are comparable to those constituting this pertinent question the Son
asked of his Father?

MY GOD, MY GOD!

The repetitions of Scripture are most impressive and instructive, but none carries the depth of anguish found in
this double exclamation. What a heart pang it suggests!
Throughout the last week before the Cross, Jesus had borne

his inexpressible agony in sublime silence of soul, but at last the climax was reached and we have this cry of his soul. We cannot view the Cross without being impressed by the strange contrasts it presents. Hands once stretched forth in blessing for the needy are now mangled and bleeding. Feet that had trodden no forbidden pathway but which were ever active on errands of mercy are now cruelly pierced. The brow upon which the dove of peace had rested (and which was anointed with gladness) is now encircled with thorns. Lips into which grace had been poured, and out of which gracious words had flowed, are now parched, cracked, and bleeding. The heart, so meek and lowly, is now broken by the soldier's sword-thrust.

Two thoughts are uppermost in the mind as we dwell upon our Lord's repeated cry:

1. *He does not say "Father" as in his first and last cry.*

He addresses him as *God.* From the age of twelve, Jesus used the endearing term, *My Father,* most frequently. Now it is, *My God.* In the Calvary Psalm (22), this appellation occurs four times. In addressing his Father as "God," Jesus appealed to divine righteousness, for God as God can only do what is right. Somehow in the darkness, he lost the consciousness of Sonship and felt thrust out into a desolate forest. Yet he clung to divine justice, for he felt that even amid the darkness God was in no way contrary to his nature.

2. *Faith clings in the darkness to a personal relationship.*

Amid all that is so hard to bear, Jesus could still say, "*My* God." Although his face was hidden, he was still *his* God. There was extreme trust in extreme trial. The remarkable aspect is that the word he used for *God* was *Eloi,* meaning, "My Strength, my strength." Being crucified in weakness, he had a deep need of strength, and received it from God who is our refuge and strength. In this Jesus left us an example to follow. If, in the hour of great sorrow, or testing, we seem to lose the consciousness of his presence, may we be found laying hold of his strength. If God's smile as the Father is eclipsed by clouds of darkness, faith can still sing—

> Thou knowest my soul dost dearly love
> The place of thine abode;
> No music drops so sweet a sound
> As these two words—MY GOD.
>   *Author Unknown*

WHY?

In the eighteenth century, Dr. Joseph Parker, minister of the City Temple in London, exercised a universal influence by his remarkable preaching and teaching of the Word. He was happily married to a beautiful wife, but one day she suddenly died, and Dr. Parker was both heartbroken and mystified. His great congregation wondered what he would preach about on the Sunday following the sad funeral. How amazed the people were when, in giving out his text, "My God, my God, why hast thou forsaken me," the griefstricken preacher said that he had been comforted in his sorrow, as he recalled that a "Why?" escaped the Savior's lips.

There was no reason that Jesus should be deserted. Why, then, was he left alone in such an hour of agony? Perhaps the answer can be found in Psalm 22:3, "But thou art holy." The prophet tells us that God is of purer eyes than to behold evil, and that he cannot look upon iniquity (Hab. 1:3). Thus the face of the Father was turned not from his Son, but from what the Son was bearing, namely, the load of the world's iniquity. God was as near as ever, but in the human consciousness of the sinbearer being made a curse for us, caused him to lose the sensible consciousness of the divine presence. As one gifted writer has so feelingly expressed it:

"He gazed across the awful gulf through which He must wade, He looked down into the horrible pit in whose depths He must struggle and up whose insurmountable sides He must painfully climb with bleeding hands and feet. He saw sins, sins, sins, pressing in on His holy body from this side and that, from behind, before, and above, and knew that as the Sin-Bearer He must bear them all and so was left alone—alone with human sin, with your sin and mine."

We greatly dishonor Jesus if we say that some of his cries in Gethsemane and Calvary were only moans of anguish stimulated by a natural fear of death. Thousands of his followers have faced a death as cruel as the Cross with quietness of resignation and a spirit of victory, with no cry whatever escaping their lips. The record of this noble band of martyrs is always inspiring, but Jesus was not dying as a martyr. Mountains upon mountains of human guilt were encircling him, and from such the Father's face was hid, as his beloved Son tasted the bitter cup of every life.

> The scourge, the thorns, the deep disgrace
> These Thou couldst bear nor once refine;
> But when Jehovah veiled His face,
> Unutterable pangs were Thine.
> *Author Unknown*

Surely an application of our Lord's cry is that it makes him our brother in mystery. Where is there a life without a *why?* At the side of an empty cradle, the heart cries *why?* Encountering blasted hopes, blighted friendships, and broken vows, we cry *why?* Have *you* reached a Calvary where you feel that God has left you? Well, remember that he is with you in the darkness, so cling to him, trust him where you cannot trace him! We live in a world of *whys* and *wherefores*. Presently we see through a glass darkly, but the paradise of revelation is ahead. Meantime, we must rest in Him who is the brother born for our adversity.

FORSAKEN

The sense of loneliness was not imaginary, but a grim reality. "Why *hast* thou forsaken me?" The pronoun *thou* made the cry more poignant. Jesus could understand traitorous Judas going out from his presence, timid Peter denying him, the disciples as a whole forsaking him. But turning to God, he cried out, "Why hast *thou,* My Father, My God, the One who called Me, 'My beloved Son,' the One who you said you delighted in, why hast *thou* forsaken me?"

Forsaken is surely one of the most tragic words in our language, for is it not the moan of a broken heart? To be *left* is sad enough, but to be *forsaken* is the crown of sorrow. The assurance Moses gave to Israel was, "The Lord thy God . . . will not fail thee, nor forsake thee" (Deut. 31:6), yet his Son felt deserted. When Jesus came to walk with men, he could say, in spite of their hostility, "I am not alone, because the Father is with me" (John 16:32). But at the Cross he appeared to be abandoned by God.

During the days of his flesh, Jesus bathed in the presence of his Father, but now his smile is withdrawn. The nails, the shame of the Cross, the cruelty of men, the insults hurled at him did not cause grief comparable to that of losing the sense of his Father's presence. The darkness of earth surrounding him was in keeping with his feeling of God-forsakenness, the worst of all darkness. It was midday when Jesus died, but Nature herself protested against man's brutal treatment of her Creator and miraculously changed midday into midnight to hide the shame of his naked, bleeding body from the gaping crowd. Denser darkness, however, covered his mind, with God's withdrawal.

Is some grievous experience ours, causing us to wonder

whether the Lord is near, or whether he hears our cry? Have we been betrayed, deserted, forsaken; and, as we pray for an explanation, do the heavens seem as brass? If so, may we hear his voice echoing through the corridors of our being, "I will never leave thee, nor forsake thee" (Heb. 13:5). Is it not wonderful to remember that Jesus was forsaken in that lone hour as he died for us, that he might promise to be with us always, even unto the hour when we receive his call, "Come up hither!"

ME

How laden with grief and disappointment is this personal pronoun! "*Me,* above all others, his well-beloved Son, who ever did those things pleasing in his sight, and who constantly glorified him on the earth!" Yet the Father left his Son to die—alone. Had he been forsaken by a cruel earth, or by angels, or by the saints in glory, then he could have borne it, but to be forsaken as the Son of God found vent in a cry of consternation as he was being tried to the limit of possibility. This is indeed a mystery our finite minds cannot fathom.

Me! Perhaps this is your irrepressible cry. With the psalmist you may be asking, "Why art thou so far from helping *me,* and from the words of *my* roaring?" *Me!* Why, I have always endeavored to live a holy life, to love his house and his people, to have my days and substance at his disposal! Then why has this heavy Cross fallen upon my shoulders? Distressed, perplexed, and sorrowing heart, you may not know the meaning of your tears as you shed them, but you will know hereafter. Presently you have the Holy Spirit as your "perpetual Comforter and eternal Inhabitant," as St. Augustine named him, and he will grace you with a quiet resignation to the divine will.

7 /

Where He Was Crucified

It is most profitable to observe that John, in his record of the crucifixion of Jesus, gives us three distinct features of the location where the tragedy yet triumph of all time was enacted.

"The place of a *skull* . . . where they crucified him" (19:17).

"The place where Jesus was crucified was nigh to the *city"* (19:20).

"In the place where he was crucified there was a garden" (19:41).

These three descriptions of the sacred place are pregnant with deep, soul-absorbing, holy truths.

A Skull indicates the depth of his humiliation, lowliness, self-abnegation, emptying on our behalf.

The City, or outside its bounds, reminds us of his rejection, reproach, unfitness to die within it.

A Garden intimates the sweet thought of victory, resurrection, compensation, joy.

THE PLACE OF A SKULL (19:17).

Calvary means "the place of a skull," and various reasons are given for such a significance. It was so-called perhaps because of the shape or formation of the place with its little rounded mound, representing the shape of a human head. The Greek term for Golgotha is "cranium." It is also affirmed that its name was derived from the fact that it was the place where criminals were killed and their bones and skulls buried.

A further thought is that the skull and bones of Jesus were not buried at this spot, for his grave was not full of dead bones. When the soldiers came to the two thieves to see if they were dead, they broke their legs. But when they came to Jesus, seeing he was dead already, they did not break his legs, thus fulfilling the prophecy: "Not one of them is broken" (Ps. 34:20; John 19:36. See Num. 9:12; Ezek. 12:46). When in his risen form he appeared to his disciples, they were frightened at his ghostlike appearance but he said, "It is I myself: handle me, and see; for a spirit hath not flesh and *bones,* as ye see me have" (Luke 24:39). Thus, when he came to ascend, he entered heaven with a complete human body, withal glorified, as the *man* Christ Jesus.

Tertullian, one of the ancient Fathers, held that it was the sacred spot where the bones of Adam were buried, and that as the blood of Jesus trickled down to the ground, it reached Adam's skull and that immediately his soul was translated to Paradise. This we do know—Jesus came to the place of death to deliver us from Adamic sin. In Adam we die; in Christ we are made alive.

But there is a more solemn implication than the mere formation and association of the spot where Jesus was crucified. It will be noted that all Four Evangelists refer to it as a "place," not as a hill, or mount. *A skull* immediately suggests emptiness, nothingness, destitution, and death. *Skull and crossbones* are the emblems of mortality. These are days when men are heady, highminded, wise in their own conceits, striving after the wisdom of this world, but not the wisdom of God. Brains, academic learning, are extolled, and often created fancied greatness, bumptiousness, and a self-opinionated attitude. With them it is *skill,* not a *skull.* Man has his reason, and thus has no need of *revelation,* which cannot teach him anything. He proudly rejects all that his much-exalted reason cannot accept, and thus scorns the humility expressed in the lines:

> That I am nothing, Thou art all
> I would be daily taught.
> *Author Unknown*

In his love and humiliation, Jesus came to "the place of a skull"—a bony structure implying nothingness, emptiness. He went bearing his Cross to Golgotha, and the greatest Cross is the parting of our own boastful greatness and sufficiency. Paul reminds us that Jesus "humbled himself," or *emptied himself* (Phil. 2:8, R.V.). This emptying process unto death implies a positive self-denial and self-humiliation. Can we say that we have reached the place of the skull, or are we, like the Gentiles, walking in the vanity of our mind? Realized nothingness comes hard. It seems beneath our dignity to sing:

> Oh, to be nothing, nothing,
> Only to lie at His feet!
> *Author Unknown*

We would much prefer to sing:

> Oh, to be something, something,
> Only to stand on our own feet!

Yet Paul would have us remember that "if a man think himself to be something, when he is nothing, he deceiveth himself" (Gal. 6:3). Of the Creator himself it is said:
"He stretcheth out the north over the empty place,
He hangeth the earth upon nothing" (Job 26:7).

NEAR THE CITY (19:20)

The second touch brings us to the inner meaning of our Lord's rejection by his own kin, by his own city and nation. Near the city, or outside of it, indicates the reproach and contempt he endured as our sin-bearer. Although the Holy One, he was not deemed fit to die in the so-called Holy City. Like the sacrifice of old, he was burned outside the camp. He suffered outside the gate (Heb. 13:10–14). The writer then goes on to exhort us to go forth unto him without the camp—he is still there—bearing his reproach. The man who gathered sticks on the Sabbath was stoned outside the camp (Num. 15:35).

Jesus was the antitype of the Jewish sacrifice, in that being the sin-offering, he must not be allowed to die within the city.

> There is a green hill far away
> Without a city wall,
> Where the dear Lord was crucified
> Who died to save us all.
> *Cecil Frances Alexander*

Does co-crucifixion with him mean participation in his isolation? Because of our witness for him, do we find ourselves unwanted, undesired, cast out from some circles? We are slow to learn that incorporation in the death of Christ carries with it his scorn and reproach. "Outside the city"—he was accustomed to the outside place from his birth when there was no room for him in the inn. Often during his ministry he had nowhere to lay his head. For us, surrender to his claims involves being on the outside of the gaieties, friendship, and pursuits alien to his holy mind and will. There are times when because of our allegiance to Jesus we find ourselves outside of some spheres of religious influence. If we are on the outside of some recognized camps, let us remember the Master is also there, so we are in the best of company. If our association with him means our separation from the kind of society we were accustomed to move in, let us cheerfully go out of such familiar surroundings into an untrodden region with the assurance that the lonely, outcast Savior is our constant Companion.

In a Garden (19:41)

What great experiences and truths revolve around the fascinating study of the gardens of Scripture! The first garden is Eden, which came fresh from the hand of God and must have been the most beautiful earth has seen. The first two chapters of Genesis describe this initial garden as a world of glory. Yet such a glorious environment did not prevent its first occupants from sinning, for Adam and Eve lost God in the garden he created for their profit and pleasure. But what the first Adam lost in garden, the last Adam by his death in a garden restored. The last book of the Bible depicts a marvelous garden of glory within a city of glory, into which sin cannot enter, for there is no more curse (Rev. 22:3, 4).

The garden John speaks of in his Gospel was the orchard or plantation belonging to Joseph who willingly surrendered it to the authorities. It was not the bare, bleak mound often given in pictures of Calvary, but a beauty spot. This is why Mary supposed the Risen Lord to be the "Gardener" (20:15). The compensating feature of the Cross, although it was the place of a skull and outside the city, is that it was near a garden. Human nature is slow to associate skulls and ashes with a fragrant, fruitful garden. Two thoughts emerge from this anomaly for us to meditate upon!

The Cross and the Garden

The world, or those who are friendly to it, may erect crosses that give us pain. Yet somehow God always arranges your Cross and mine to be in a garden. He can make us fruitful even in a land of affliction. Our Golgotha and the garden go together. Palms and willows, sorrow and joy are intermingled. If you have entered the fellowship of his sufferings and are now in death-union with Jesus, look out for the garden. Do not allow the Cross to obliterate the garden, otherwise the isolation and shame of an isolated life will fill you with sadness. Think of the gain of a life completely identified with the Cross—the flowers of grace and the fruits of the Spirit! The seed dies, but in dying, it produces a rich and fruitful garden.

Death and Life

Christ's death and burial in a garden may have suggested the idea of adorning graves with flowers and plants. The blooming flowers around his Cross and tomb were prophetic heralds of his resurrection. Flowers springing from the dead earth typified his higher, fuller life beyond. It may seem gruesome and contradictory for blood to be found dripping from a Cross in a beautiful spot like this. Does it seem as if your garden is being spoiled by the crimson-dyed, ugly-shaped Cross? May the Lord, then, open your eyes to see that it is only adorning and adding to the fragrance of your garden! Suffering produces flowers of richer hues. "From the ground there blossoms red, life that shall endless be."

For the Savior, the Cross in a garden meant joy, victory,

compensation in a glorious harvest of souls, and the earnest of paradise, with its tree of life, and twelve manner of fruits. If your life has been emptied of its self-glory, dependence, efforts, will, wisdom, and advancement, and you find yourself rejected, despised, unwanted in the world, even by those from whom you expected sympathy, ever think of him who died in a garden. As the tomb was in a garden, so bury your self-reputation (and what others may say, think or do) deep in Christ's grave, then go out bearing the aroma of the garden of resurrection, ever singing:

> Like a watered garden,
> Full of fragrance rare;
> Lingering in Thy presence,
> Let my life appear.
> *E. May Grimes*

*Save thyself, and come down from
the cross. . . . descend now from
the cross (Mark 15:30, 32).*

8 /

A Christ without a Cross

"Throned upon the awful tree." This is how the death
of Christ has been beautifully and truthfully described, seeing he reigns from the tree. His Cross led to his Crown.
Crucifixion led to the coronation of him who became our
Substitute. Through his foes, he reached his throne; and
in glory he ever wears the insignia of royalty in his scars.
Those "rich wounds, still visible above," are admired by
all of heaven's adoring host. Yet, although the Cross is the
wisdom of God, it is foolishness in the eyes of men who,
like the Pharisees of old, want a Christ without his Cross,
but both were nailed together.

The supposedly religious people of his day were the chief
priests. Just as do those of our day who are religious, but
certainly not Christian, they wanted a Christ without his
grim and shameful Cross. They do not want the mangled,
bleeding, dying form of the One who suffered for lost, hell-
deserving sinners, and they try to expunge the Cross from
their theology as being too repugnant for the fine and cultured taste of man. Away with such a gospel of shambles!
But no Cross, no Christ—no death, no deliverance—no Gol-

gotha, no glory—no blood, no blessing—no atonement, no access. Let us try to examine more closely this attitude toward Christ and his Cross.

FALSE HONOR: "Christ the King of Israel" (Mark 15:32)

Not only were the chief priests heartlessly cruel in the death to which they brought Christ, but also in the spirit of mockery seen in their use of this august title used to assail him with hypocritical lips. If he was their king, then why make him die for such a claim?

Let Christ

He came as the Messiah, God's anointed and sent One, but his foes would not own him as such. When Jesus asked of Peter, "Whom say ye that I am?" his reply was, "Thou art the Christ, the Son of the living God." Then he said, "Blessed art thou, Simon Barjona: for flesh and blood hath not revealed it unto thee, but my Father which is in heaven" (Matt. 16:15–17). The conception of Jesus as the promised Messiah can only come by divine revelation, an avenue of which the chief priests were ignorant. No matter what men call him, theirs is the language of mockery unless they have a revelation from heaven. If we have experienced the efficacy of his blood, and the inspiration of the Spirit, then we have no doubt about him being *The Lord Jesus Christ.* No man can call him such, but by the Spirit. Without such a revelation, men may try to honor him, but their hearts are far from him.

The King of Israel

Jesus was born as Israel's king, yet the priests flung the taunt at him, "What a strange king you are! Where is your power?" But this despised and rejected One, dying like a criminal, was indeed God's appointed Ruler. The Jews wanted him, in the zenith of his influence as king, to take the kingdom by force, and not to talk about dying on a Cross. They wanted him on a throne, not on a tree of shame. This desire continues, for even today there are those religious leaders who want to take him down from a Cross and give him honor as a teacher, social reformer, or model to live by. But such is false honor, if Calvary is belittled. We have no Christ but the One, crucified for us. We have not to preach *Christ* and stop there, as some do, but "Christ, and him crucified," as Paul loved to do.

DIABOLICAL TREATMENT: "With him they crucify two thieves" (15:27)

The context reveals that men hate the Cross because it shows them how low and base human nature has fallen. Calvary displays the greatest love on the part of God, and the greatest hate on the part of the sinner. How can we speak about the divine in man after the bloody spectacle of the Cross?

Shame and Suffering

When the priests gloated over Christ's position between two thieves, they classified him as being the vilest of the vile, with no more value than his companions in anguish, who were dying for their crimes. Where do we place him? We crucify him anew—don't be shocked—when we put him between two thieves, namely, sin in an evil heart, and a godless world all around without, thinking more of sin and the world than the Savior.

Derision and Death

We read that the priests mocked, the passers-by railed, and, at the first, both thieves reviled. Diabolical treatment was received by one and all. They scorned because Jesus was on the Cross apparently helpless to save himself in spite of his claims to Kingship. There are still those who mock and revile at the presentation of a Christ crucified. The Cross is ever gruesome to unbelief. It was so to the cultured Greeks of Paul's day who thought his preaching of the Cross to be foolishness. Yet, as the apostle goes on to say, "It pleased God by the foolishness of preaching to save them who believe" (1 Cor. 1:21). It was not foolish preaching that he blessed, but the foolishness of the truth they proclaimed, namely, Christ on a Cross bleeding, dying for a lost world. We know Golgotha was an ugly scene, but the message it presents makes for beauty in the lives of those who believe that it is the power of God unto salvation.

BLIND UNBELIEF: "That we may see and believe" (Mark 15:32)

Those callous priests wanted a display of miraculous power before accepting the claims of Christ to be their Messiah. But he never performed miracles to satisfy idle curiosity, or even for his own needs. The Gospels reveal an economy of power. The world's axiom is, "Seeing is believing," which the priests accepted when they said that we may see and believe. Faith's attitude is the reverse, "Believing is seeing." "Blessed are they that have not seen, and yet have believed" (John 20:29). Let us hasten to say, however, that because he was the Son of God with power, Jesus could have miraculously stepped down from his Cross, healed his wounds, and scattered his foes, thus making them see in order to believe. But he voluntarily remained crucified. He *endured* the cross and despised its shame (Heb. 12:2).

The Savior did not descend in response to blind unbelief, or a presumptuous God-dethroning attitude. He remains on his Cross until he is received as the Redeemer, then he makes the believing heart his throne. He did not satisfy the craving for the spectacular. It was imperative for him to stay there for these three reasons:

He could not disobey the Father. Had he not already declared, "Not my will, but thine be done"? To die as he was, then, was God's will, and he accepted such with delight.

He could not break the Scriptures. Mark says that by his death "the scripture was fulfilled" (Mark 15:28). It had been already prophesied that as the Messiah he would be "cut off" (Dan. 6:26. See Isa. 53:9–12). If, then, he had complied with the blatant request to come down from the Cross, he would have nullified God's eternal truth.

He could not allow man to perish. Without the shedding of blood, there could have been no remission of sin, and so the curse was placed upon him and he bore it. He did not save himself, in order that he might save others. Nails never kept him fastened to the tree, but love for the perishing, and the passion to redeem them from sin.

UNWANTED CROSS: "Come down from the Cross" (Mark 15:30)

It is well to examine the reasons why some people prefer a crossless Christ in the present, evil days. Why they desire a Savior without sacrifice—love, but not blood—glory but not a gibbet—religion but not a Redeemer. We are living in times when even some preachers are becoming all too silent regarding all the Cross involves. Why is this crimson gospel rejected?

1. *It reveals the heart of man.* The Cross exposes guilt and unmasks man's hatred of holiness. It was there that

man did his worst and revealed his inert hatred to Christ, as God's ideal for man.

2. *It declares the purpose of God.* God gave his Son to die, for there was no other way of life, no other method of destroying the works of the devil. Calvary is a huge blunder, if man by himself can satisfy the claims of a righteous God. The Cross reveals the need of a Substitute, of atonement by blood as the only means of access to God. There are many ways by which a man can be lost, but only *one* way by which he can be saved, namely, by the crimson stream. To be delivered from sin only through the blood may be humbling to the pride of the human heart, and rejected by the self-confident, deceitful mind, but the Cross stands as man's only refuge from divine wrath and condemnation.

3. *It presents a pattern of life.* As we require Christ on the Cross to save us, and to satisfy God's demands on our behalf, is it not blessed to know that both purposes were nailed together, and that through eternity the Savior will bear the scars of a completed contract? If we accept him, we must accept his Cross, for there is no other way by which we can be delivered from this present evil world and live as those who are dead to it. There are those who know in their heart of hearts what God wants, but they smother his voice and their conscience because of their unwillingness to pay the price of a thoroughly saved and sanctified life.

There is no such person as a crossless Christian even as there is no crossless Christ. As he is, so are we in this world. If, by faith, we appropriate a crucified Savior, we must be prepared to take up his Cross and follow him, as Simon had to do (Mark 15:21). In practice, this means living the crucified life as Paul teaches in Galatians 6. We must bear the scars of separation from the world, flesh and the devil, and if we are true to Christ and his Cross, the world and some religious people will not be long in showing their hatred. If we would reign in life, the only way is by death to the world's allurements. Jesus offers you what your sin gave him, namely, a Cross, and if you accept it, and by his grace live the crucified life for the sake and glory of him who stayed on his Cross, then, you, too, will share in the power of his resurrection.

9 /

Earth's Most Sacred Spot

Scripture is eloquent with the truth that experiences sanctify places. The *certain place* Jacob lighted upon when he left home, and tarried all night, was to become the most remarkable and unforgettable place in his career. It was there that he had the vision of God's plan for his life, and the assurance of divine presence and provision for the future. Overawed by the revelation he received, the patriarch exclaimed, "Surely the Lord is in this place. . . . How dreadful is this place . . . this is the gate of heaven" (Gen. 28:16, 17). With ourselves, places stand out because of happy or sorrowful relationships and associations. It was so in Christ's life, in which several places are prominent as a range of mountain peaks, and in which mixed experiences were his.

There is Bethlehem, the place of his wonderful, mysterious birth—the place all tourists to the Holy Land are eager to visit, and at which they bow in reverence as they think of him who became God manifest in flesh.

There is Nazareth, the place of his early training in home and school, and in which it took God thirty years to equip his Son for only three years of ministry. God is never in any hurry when it comes to the preparation of those he desires to use in a mighty way.

There is Jerusalem, the place of his worship and hopes, yet a place over which he came to weep because of its rejection of him and of his protecting care.

There is Galilee, the place in and around which much of his ministry was exercised. What memorable experiences are associated with the Galilean lake!

There is Bethany, the place to which Jesus retreated for fellowship and rest.

There is Gethsemane, the place, most awesome, because of his intercession and conflict, and yet triumph—a place most holy, for its ground was soaked with his bloody sweat.

There is Olivet, the place most blessed for it witnessed his compassion, his ascension, and is linked to his return for his own.

There is Calvary, the place of his resignation, his isolation, and his redemption for mankind. It is to this place so central in human history that we now turn our attention.

The Weeping Place for Sin

How drenched the earth became with human tears! What liquid anguish was manifested there! The prophet of old had said, "They shall look upon him whom they pierced, and they shall mourn for him" (Zech. 12:10); and at the Cross a great company bewailed and lamented him, and the daughters of Jerusalem wept for him. Those who beheld the sight of Jesus dying, smote their breasts (Luke 23:27, 28, 40). Centuries ago in England, several towns erected cross-beams in the marketplace which they called *weeping crosses.* The people were urged to go home by the weeping cross, and tarrying at such to confess and repent of their sins. But the nature of tears is twofold:

Tears of sympathy. Such were the kind the women shed,

and they were exhorted by Jesus not to weep over his suffering, but to weep for themselves and their offspring because of the dark days ahead. Art, literature, poetry, and music reach their highest heights when they depict the Cross in such a way as to move our hearts.

> Thus might I hide my blushing face,
>   While His dear Cross appears,
> Dissolve my heart in thankfulness,
>   And melt mine eyes to tears.
>   *Isaac Watts*

Mere drops of grief, however, can never repay the debt we owe him for all he willingly suffered in our stead. Dark Calvary calls for the dropping of warm tears from the heart, and not for a sloppy emotionalism.

Tears of penitence. They were the kind Peter shed when he went out from his Lord's presence after denying him and "wept bitterly" (Luke 22:62). Sympathetic tears are meaningless unless they result in penitential tears. Have you ever wept, not only over the record of the kind of death Jesus died, but for the fact that he died for *you?* As Elizabeth Cecilia Clephane expresses it in her most unique hymn, *Beneath the Cross of Jesus:*

> Upon that Cross of Jesus:
>   Mine eye at times can see
> The very dying form of One
>   Who suffered there for me;
> And from my stricken heart, with tears,
>   Two wonders I confess—
> The wonders of redeeming love,
>   And my own worthlessness.

THE TRYSTING PLACE OF PEACE

What a great and glorious truth Paul expresses in his Ephesian Letter, "That he might reconcile both unto God

in one body by the cross" (2:16). Then we have his further
revelation: "Having made peace through the blood of his
cross, by him to reconcile all things unto himself" (Col.
1:20, 21). The Cross, then, is the trysting place between
God and the sinner, "O trysting place, where Heaven's love
and Heaven's justice meet." Thrice holy in himself, God
could not contact the unholy. Had he not decreed, "The
soul that sinneth, it shall die"? How, then, was the yawning
gulf between to be bridged? The Cross solved the problem.
God gave, Christ came and died as our Substitute, and the
Spirit effects the reconciliation between God and the sinner.
Through the Cross we are now at peace with God, and
we have his peace within our hearts. "Through him we
both have access by one Spirit unto the Father" (Eph. 2:18).
In this great passage all the Trinity are involved in the
work of redemption.

God in holiness meets me at Calvary, and I in my sinfulness meet him there; and as I pray, "God be merciful to
me a sinner" (Luke 18:13), the miracle of reconciliation is
effected. At the Cross mercy and truth meet together, and
righteousness and peace kiss each other. Judas knew this
trysting place, but it had no effect upon him. Happy are
we if we can sing with Horatius Bonar—

> I hear the words of love,
>   I gaze upon the blood;
> I see the mighty sacrifice,
>   And I have peace with God.

The Hiding Place from Judgment

Moses supplies us with a fitting illustration of the benefits
of the Cross when he describes the Lord passing through
the land of Egypt in judgment. All the first-born of man
and beast were smitten with death, except those whose
homes were sprinkled with blood: "When he seeth the blood

upon the lintel, and on the two side posts, the Lord will pass over the door, and will not suffer the destroyer to come into your houses to smite you" (Exod. 12:23).

If the blood shed by Jesus at Calvary is upon us and our children, then our home is eternally safe and secure. The Cross is the only shelter from the penalty and power of sin, and we are indeed blessed if we are hiding in the smitten Rock of Ages. Satan and satanic forces can only be overcome by the blood of the lamb (Rev. 12:11). If our life is hid with Christ in God, then we are free from all condemnation, and the crucified life is not a second blessing but the other half of the gift already received by faith.

> O safe and blessed shelter,
> O refuge tried and sweet.
> *E. C. Clephane*

Shelter, also, from coming doom is provided by his blood. The only hearts assured of heaven are those washed in the blood of the Lamb (Rev. 5:9, 10; 7:14).

THE BIRTHPLACE OF LOVE

Some of the old divines were wont to call the Cross *The Academy of Love.*

> Inscribed upon the Cross we see,
> In shining letters, "God is love."
> *Author Unknown*

As I have said before, the Cross was not the cause of God's love, but the effect of his love. Jesus did not die to make God love us, but because he did love us. "God so loved the world, that he gave his only begotten Son" (John 3:16).

The birthplace of our love to him

It is as the Man of Calvary that he won our hearts. By
the Spirit we were brought to love God, because he first
loved us (1 John 4:19. See 4:10). The Cross claims the affection of the young because as an unknown poet expressed
it he was:

> Dead ere His prime.
> Not one golden hair was gray
> Upon His crucifixion day.

Jesus was not a decrepit old man when he died, but the
young Prince of Glory, only thirty-three years of age.

The birthplace of our love to believers

When his love is shed abroad in our hearts, we love one
another, and the nearer we live to the Cross, the nearer
we are to each other. If hearts are filled with Calvary's
love, what a mighty force the household of faith becomes.
If you are not as near to, and loving, as you should be
toward a fellow-believer, take a fresh look at him who came
as God's love-gift for you.

The birthplace of our love for sinners

The greatest need of a lost world is for more Calvary
hearts. There would be fewer sinners in the world if only
more of us, professing to be saved by Christ's death, had
Calvary's love and passion for the lost. If God gave his
Son to die for the world, then how can we, how dare we,
be indifferent about the millions, at home and abroad, still
in their sin, and who, if they die in it, die lost forevermore?
A story is told of William Burns, the renowned Scottish

saint and missionary. One day, while home on furlough in his native Glasgow, he was walking down its Sauchihall Street. So overcome was he by the crowds passing up and down, that he ran up an alleyway and falling on his knees cried, "O God, so many Christless souls, they break my heart!" May God stir us, by all means, to save some.

THE RESTING PLACE OF FAITH

It is a personal faith that makes the possible, actual, in one's experiences. "If we believe," the Cross becomes effective in our lives. A strong faith in a wrong object will never save, but even a weak faith in a right object will. See 1 Peter 1:21. It is not the strength of our faith that saves, but the power of the blood upon which our faith is centered. How secure we are if we can sing:

> My soul has found a resting place,
> And I am now through heavenly grace,
> At peace with God.
> *Author Unknown*

10 /

The Message All-Supreme

One of the most striking features of the Bible is its ability to express the maximum of truth in the minimum of words. It is never guilty of mere verbiage. The most fitting words are chosen, and the message set forth in clear, crisp, short sentences which none can fail to understand. Paul was a genius in such condensation. Thus, in four words he declares the gospel of Golgotha: *Christ died for us.* The apostle leaves us in no doubt as to the identification of those implied in the pronoun, "us," for in a previous verse he wrote, "Christ died for the ungodly" (Rom. 5:6). The great truth of redemption is summarized in the four words consolidating the message all-supreme.

THE PERSON WHO DIED: "Christ"

The original of this title, as used by Paul, carries a slight emphasis, as if pointing to the wonder of such a Divine Person dying in such a way, and who, because of his dignity and honor, gave efficacy to his death. The death of the two thieves crucified with Christ was unavailing for others because of their character and nature. He was sinless; they were not; hence the frank confession, "We indeed justly; for we receive the due reward of our deeds: but this man hath done nothing amiss" (Luke 23:41). That Christ, holy, harmless, and undefiled should die for the ungodly, caused Paul to marvel. To think that he, above all others, the preexistent Lord, Creator of the world, the God-Man, the only Perfect Man the world has ever known should die on a Cross, was the wonder of wonders to the apostle. Christ had no sin of his own to die for—he had no stain upon his character. He ever wore the white flower of a blameless life. He had no ungodly trait in his nature and no blemish whatever in or upon his life. Yet this was the One who was made sin for us. What else could even angels do, but veil their faces in the presence of such love?

THE DEATH HE DIED: "Died"

What a tragic little word this is! Yet what hope for a lost world is wrapped up in such a stupendous mystery. The Lord of Life died; the Everlasting Father died; the King Eternal came from glory to Golgotha, from a throne to thorns, from eternity to a grave. Man's hope of eternal life depends upon the One who died. Mark, it does not say, "Christ lived for the ungodly." There is no salvation for them in the example of the lovely life of the Lord Jesus, although such added virtue to his death. This was the death sentence pronounced upon those who had broken the law of God, and the sinless and unsinning One who made the dread sentence his own. This is why there is emphasis by position in the Greek of Paul's *multum in parvo:* "Christ—for the ungodly—died." Such a dark and awful death has a twofold implication:

1. *It was the supreme requirement of the law.* God demanded death for disobedience, and his Son, obedient unto

death, even the death of the Cross, met the demand, fully and finally, for the disobedient (Gen. 3:3; Phil. 2:8). Having paid the uttermost farthing to the divine requirement, Christ forever freed us from condemnation.

> The soul that sinneth dies.
>   My awful doom I heard.
> I was forever lost,
>   But for Thy gracious Word.
>   *Author Unknown*

And that gracious, all-glorious word is: "Christ died for us."

2. *It was the supreme proof of divine love.* Sovereign loving kindness is at the foundation of the death of the Cross. It was there that love reached its limit. Though they were stiff-necked, hard-hearted, rebellious, and unworthy creatures, these were those of whom it is said, "Yea, he loved the people" (Deut. 33:3). All the rays of God's love are centered in Jesus as the Substitute for sinners. He left his Father's bosom, came to earth, and gave his blood and his life for sinners, and so he redeemed them to God. What glorious mystery of infinite and eternal love the Cross reveals! May the Lord direct our hearts into this sacrificial love of his!

> O love of unexampled kind!
> That leaves all thought so far behind:
> Where length, and breadth, and depth,
>   and height,
> Are lost to my astonished sight:
> Lord shed abroad that love of Thine
> In this poor sinful soul of mine.
>   *Author Unknown*

THE WAY HE DIED: "FOR"

Having dealt briefly with this preposition—one small word containing an ocean of truth—let us now, with adoring hearts, examine it more closely. This simple word expresses a relationship between things or persons, and in the context it is related to a decreed death and the ungodly. The two outstanding meanings of the word are well-known. The original, *huper,* used by Paul so often in his Epistles, signifies a deep truth. It suggests a bending over to protect as a mother bird will cover her young at the sacrifice of her own life. I once read of a fire that destroyed a farm, and a search among the debris revealed a dead, charred hen, with a brood of live chicks beneath her. The Hebrew word is *kaphar,* meaning, to protect by means of covering, and this is what Christ made possible for us when and as he died on our behalf. Acting as our Representative, he secured for us a present and eternal salvation.

Then there is the further word, *anti,* signifying "instead of." Speaking of saints as ambassadors, Paul exhorted the Corinthians: "We pray you in Christ's stead, be ye reconciled to God" (2 Cor. 5:20). The same thought is found in the great verse, "Who for—*instead of*—the joy set before him endured the cross" (Heb. 12:2, added italics mine for emphasis). Here we have the substitutionary aspect of his death, which brings us to the heart of the supreme message: "Christ died for—*instead of*—the ungodly." His death was not only voluntary, but vicarious in that he tasted death instead of every man. One wonders if Barabbas caught this inner substitutionary aspect as he gazed upon the Cross he should have died on. Did he look up at the bloodstained face, and cry, "O Christ, you died instead of me!"?

For Whom He Died: "Us"

The proper rendering of the apostle's affirmation is, "Christ died for (us) the ungodly" (Rom. 5:6, 8). Going back, Paul speaks of faith justifying the ungodly, but implies certain limitations (Rom. 4:5), but here he is describing the worst among the sinful. The designation was inclusive and covered Paul and all mankind ruined by the Fall, and throws into contrast, the holiness of the Substitute, and the hellishness of the sinner—the best for the worst and the brightest for the blackest. Christ and the ungodly, how far apart—yet they meet at the Cross and are made one. Paul made the atonement personal when he wrote, "He loved me, and gave himself for me." Having caught the full vision of the Cross, he vowed, "I will very gladly spend and be spent for—on behalf of—you" (2 Cor. 12:15). The margin has it, "spend and spent out." Christ was not only willing to spend, but to be spent out, for he gave the last drop of his blood for our redemption, and Paul came to experience the fellowship of such suffering. May our life and lips ever proclaim this message supreme: *Christ died for us!*

11 /

A Tree As a Throne

Among the Psalms, Psalm 96 is most outstanding in that it is a great missionary Psalm, revealing Israel's responsibility to make Jehovah known among the nations, so that they might form the world empire of such a king. There is a difference between a king and an emperor, in that a king is the chief ruler in and over one nation, while an emperor is the highest title of a sovereign who rules over nations and lesser sovereigns. Christ as the Lord of Lords and King of Kings is the World-Emperor for whom the world awaits. The day is coming when the kingdoms of this world will become his world-kingdom (Rev. 11:15).

The tenth verse of Psalm 96 is practically at the center of the Psalms and is therefore full of deep, spiritual significance. As an earthly sovereign reigns from a throne, the Lord has his throne—a blood-red one. The A.V. ends, "The Lord reigneth," but an old Latin Version reads, "The Lord reigneth from the tree." All crucifixes before the eleventh century portrayed Christ robed and crowned. Justin Martyr accused the Jews of erasing the addition, "from the tree," from the original because of their hatred toward Christ as the promised Messiah. But the words were cherished through the centuries as a prediction of the Cross, and thus, when Christ came into the world it was as the King of the Jews (Matt. 2:2). The throne, however, from which he rules the nations, and our hearts, is not a gilded one, but gory, even the Cross of Calvary. An old Latin hymn has the stanza:

> Fulfilled is all that David told
> In true prophetic song of old
> Amid the nations God saith He
> Hath reigned and triumphed from the Tree.

Another hymnist renders it:

> The truth that David learned to sing,
> Its deep fulfilment here attains.
> Tell all the earth the Lord is King!
> Lo, from the Cross a King He reigns.
> *Author Unknown*

John Ellerton has the couplet:

> Throned upon the awful Tree,
> King of grief, I watch with Thee.

In the realm of grace, Christ reigns from his Cross. On the tree he was Victor, not Victim. The dying Savior was the triumphant Lord, and his sovereignty can be found in his last utterances, for seven times his parched lips opened amidst the awful conflict of the Cross. It is not without reason that the number chosen is *seven,* signifying completeness, and thus expressive of his supremacy or sovereignty in the realm of grace.

The progress of the seven cries is Christlike in that they begin with his enemies and end with himself. All through his life it was others first, self last. There is therefore no preacher like the dying Christ; no pulpit like the Cross; no congregation like those around the Cross; no sermon like the seven sayings:

1. SOVEREIGN GRACE: "Father, forgive them; for they know not what they do" (Luke 23:34).

The first action of Jesus after he was nailed to the Cross was to pray for the forgiveness of those who put him there. Quickly he made intercession for his transgressors. Pardon was sought for them in virtue of the blood now freely flowing. What supreme magnanimity! How kingly and kind to seek the forgiveness of his enemies. What a triumph it was to pray in deep agony of body and to feel the Fatherhood of God, and Jesus felt it. And he pleaded for forgiveness from a fatherly heart. When he was in the morning of his life, at the age of twelve, his heart was warmed by the thought of his Father's love. Now in black midnight, faith did not fail and he was still able to say, *Father!* Has he not left us an example to emulate? Are we not exhorted to be tender-hearted, forgiving one another, even as God for Christ's sake has forgiven us?

2. SOVEREIGN POWER: "Today shalt thou be with me in paradise" (Luke 23:43).

An unforgettable aspect of the Crucifixion is the storylike flower of beauty amongst those dreary crags of agony and seas of blood. Robert Browning reminds us that, " 'Twas a thief that said the last kind word to Christ!" At the very depth of Christ's suffering, one of the malefactors had a revelation of him as a king, and in spite of all the mocking and scorning, exalted him and prayed for a place in his kingdom. Others might spurn his claim to kingship, but this pardoned rebel recognized it and sought to be with the king. He became the first sinner to enter paradise washed in the blood of the Lamb—the first subject of the new kingdom of grace.

Jesus was not too absorbed with his own agonies as to forget the dire spiritual need of his sin-stained fellow sufferer. He was a king indeed, for although his hand was nailed to the tree, it was yet able to open the door of paradise to a believing soul and enter in there with the king himself. It is sad, when in our self-centeredness, with our own Cross filling our vision, compassion for others is obscured. We have the Calvary heart when we bury our own grief and go out to other sorrow-stricken souls in dire need of a forgiving Savior's love and mercy.

3. SOVEREIGN LOVE: "Woman, behold thy Son! . . . Behold thy mother" (John 19:26, 27).

Here Jesus turns from the outer circle of the sin-blinded Jews and a repentant thief, to the inner circle of those nearest his heart, in need of consolation. He addresses his beloved mother and the disciple he loved. Tenderly he commended them to each other. Truly, in this act, the Master reigned in thoughtfulness and consideration for those dear to him, as he dies. What supremacy! The hour of death has been described as—

> That dark hour when bands remove
> And none are named but names of love.
> *Author Unknown*

In his dying moments, Jesus was concerned about the future of the woman who had borne him, now her soul was pierced with the sword. Out of deep poverty he had already made precious gifts—to his murderers he bequeathed the forgiveness of God—to his companion in crucifixion, the prospect and pleasure of paradise. Now to his mother and his friend,

John, his two most precious treasures on earth, he bequeaths one to the other. He had no money or possessions to leave Mary, for he brought nothing into the world, and had nothing to give as he passed out of it. But he gave a son to his mother, and a mother to his much-loved disciple who was probably motherless. In this thoughtless, cruel, and ungrateful age of ours, let us resolve to manifest the same kingly grace to the forlorn.

4. SOVEREIGN SACRIFICE: "My God, my God, why hast thou forsaken me?" (Matt. 27:46).

Having previously dealt with this fourth cry from the Cross more fully, a brief note or two of further reflection is all that is necessary here. Now Jesus comes nearer still and speaks to none save God; and man will never be able to fathom the mystery prompting such a question of anguish. It was an hour of dense darkness, for the natural light of the world was going out, and the darkness overtaking the Savior's spirit speaks of his crucifixion of heart. At that moment he felt the terribleness of the load of human sin and such a weight of iniquity made his Cross so heavy, for his God to whom he cried could not look upon sin and iniquity.

As we think of "Emmanuel's orphaned cry," there comes to mind his confession while ministering among men, "I am not alone, because the Father is with me" (John 16:32). But now he feels alone and without his Father's presence. Yet he stayed there and endured that God-forsaken grief that we might be saved by his matchless grace. Perhaps he heard God repeat the very words he had used to comfort his disciples in a time of perplexity, for the consolation of his Son, "What I do thou knowest not; but thou shalt know hereafter" (John 13:7). But assurance of the Father's presence returned, for as he died he cried, "Father, into thy hands I commend my spirit" (Luke 23:46). Ours is the privilege because of all he endured, never to be forsaken by him.

5. SOVEREIGN HUMILIATION: "I thirst" (John 19:28).

As the tide of anguish assuaged, Jesus was able to realize what he had endured. For some twenty hours he had not tasted anything, and for about six hours he had been hanging on the tree. The soldiers gave him vinegar to drink, but he would not take anything until he had accomplished all that had been prophesied regarding the purpose of his travail. Possibly Satan plied him with the old temptation, "Command waters to quench your thirsty lips."

> His are the thousand sparkling rills
> Which from a thousand fountains burst,
> And fill with music all the hills,
>   He cries—I thirst.
>   *Author Unknown*

He could have satisfied his own thirst, for he created all streams and wells, but he endured a bitter, burning, raging thirst in his determination never to swerve from his Father's will. Yet he was never so kingly as when he revealed his humanity in his cry for water. What a distance he traveled in the humbling of himself. He had a twofold thirst apart from this one to which he gave utterance, namely, the thirst for the accomplishment of the divine will, and a thirst for righteousness which brings with it the benediction of God (Matt. 5:6). With the psalmist, Jesus prayed, "My soul thirsteth for God." Can we say that we share his thirst?

6. SOVEREIGN PROVISION: "It is finished" (John 19:30).

What triumph! What a paean of victory! Can we not detect the shout of a Victor as this acclamation leaves his parched throat? By dying, death he slew. The Cross was his ruddy throne, for the foe of his Father (and of the faithful) was defeated thereon. Salvation was procured for all mankind. Deliverance for the sin-bound was his finished work. " 'Tis done, the great transaction's done," and all that is required of a sinner is the willingness to repent of his sin and, by faith, accept the full salvation the Cross procured for all mankind. May grace be ours to become more kingly in completion! Too often our lives are strewn with unfinished tasks and ragged edges. Like the man in the parable, we began to build but were not able to finish.

7. SOVEREIGN TRUST: "Father, into thy hands I commend my spirit" (Luke 23:46).

The phrase, "he gave up the ghost," means he dismissed his spirit. While it seemed as if men had taken his life, actually he gave it. And now there was the voluntary committal of his spirit to God. He could have died sooner had he wished, but he kept alive until he drained the cup of its bitter dregs. His life had been one of trust, now he dies in trust. He died as he had lived, committing himself to God. "Trust in God," says Faber, "is the last of all things, and the whole of all things." Is this not the way for us to live and die, believing that God is able to keep all we commit to him? If we would reign in life we must constantly commit our way unto the Lord.

Are we learning to make our Cross a throne—not falling under it, but reigning from it? Christina Rossetti has the stanza—

> Nailed to the racking Cross, then bed of down
>   More dear, whereon to stretch Myself and sleep;
> So did I win a Kingdom—Share My crown
>   A harvest—Come and reap.

How fearful it is to fall into the hands of the Lord God, to be dragged out of life with sin on the soul! Better far to rest in his fatherly hands and at death go home to him, even as Jesus did.

12 /

The Lamb and His Load

This marvelous, well-known verse reveals how familiar John the Baptist was with Old Testament types and prophecies setting forth the person and the work of Christ. Doubtless as he spoke of Christ in this way, he was thinking of the processes leading from ancient lambs to *the* Lamb, and of the gradual unfolding of the redemptive plan from Abel's lamb to Christ. The question of the Old Testament is, "Where is the Lamb?" and the answer is found in John's exclamation, "Behold the Lamb of God!" (Gen. 22:7; John 1:36). The figure of the *Lamb* was a favorite with the apostle John who uses it thirty-one times in *The Revelation.* And the word he used means "the little lamb," in contrast to the Beast, so great and wild. This blessed evangelical utterance of the Baptist falls into two sections, The Lamb and His Load, or The Bearer and His Burden. In the love and provision of God, the Lamb and His Load became mysteriously mingled on our behalf.

THE LAMB: "Behold the Lamb of God"

There are several deep truths wrapped up in this arresting title worth tarrying over. For instance, the exclamation, *Behold,* always precedes some deep truth, as found in the plea of Jesus, "Behold, I stand at the door and knock" (Rev. 3:20). In like manner, his forerunner fastens upon the word to draw attention to the unique unfolding of the Person and Purpose of Christ.

1. *His Nature:* THE LAMB

The is a definite article and implies that all Old Testament lambs typified Christ as the perfect, paschal Lamb. He alone is the great Lamb whose sacrifice is efficacious to redeem lost sinners and is thus a fitting emblem seeing he came to complete all the ancient sacrifices, types, and symbols.

There was his innocence. A child untried, never tested, and ignorant of the gross sins of life is called "an innocent child." But Christ's innocence was of a different caliber. His was an innocent holiness he never lost in spite of fierce, satanic temptation. His life remained unsoiled, just as sunbeams never contact the dirt they shine through. Living and laboring in a sinful world, he remained holy, harmless, and undefiled, and separate from sinners in respect to sin. True, he became sin for us, but he never became a sinner. Had he sinned he would have forfeited the right to function as our Savior. It is because he remained sinless that he can save. The lambs offered of old were innocent because they had no consciousness or knowledge of evil. But Christ had a deep knowledge of sin, yet ever refused its seductive charms and challenged his foes to convict him of any committed sin. In him, that is within his flesh, there dwelt nothing but good things, hence his virtue as the slain Lamb.

There was no other good enough,
  To pay the price of sin:
He only could unlock the gate of Heaven,
  And let us in.
              Cecil Frances Alexander

There was his gentleness. In Sunday school we learned to sing, "Gentle Jesus, meek and mild"—and he was all this in the days of his flesh. If, as the proverb expresses it, "Gentleness is invincible," then it is this virtue that has made him, "Strong Son of God, immortal Love." This is the gentleness that makes us great (2 Sam. 22:36). The lamb is known as a meek, unmurmuring animal. It is therefore a fitting type of Jesus as the Lamb of God. His meekness, however, must not be mistaken for weakness. We read, do we not, of "the *wrath* of the Lamb" (Rev. 6:16), and he cannot be indifferent to sin, or condone evil. Shakespeare has the phrase:

Your gentleness shall force
More than your force move us to gentleness.

Did not Jesus himself say that "the meek . . . shall inherit the earth" (Matt. 5:5)? Because of his gentleness, the earth will yet be filled with his glory. The meek Lamb is to be the King of kings.

There was his submission. Lambs never complain as they are led to the slaughterhouse—they cannot, seeing they are destitute of our human understanding and personality. They may not know it but they exist for others, their wool providing our raiment, and their flesh, our food. In Old Testament times, lambs were often forced or dragged to the altar, but God's Lamb was no unwilling victim for he gave himself freely for us. He was led as a lamb to his death, because he knew his sacrifice was to benefit a lost world. Martyrs and covenanters were forced to die, but Jesus chose death—

it did not claim him. Willingly, he tasted death for every man. His whole life was one of voluntary sacrifice. We often say of some hard and grievous experience, "If I had known what was to come my way, I could never have faced it." But Jesus knew every step of the blood-red way as he walked the whole road with bleeding feet to a Cross on which he was to die for others. F. R. Havergal in one of her matchless poems exclaims—

> King of Eternity! what revelation
>   Could the created and finite sustain,
> But for Thy marvelous manifestation,
>   Godhead incarnate in weakness and pain!

2. *His Relationhip:* OF GOD

Jesus was no common, ordinary man, as a lamb chosen from among many belonging to an Israelite was brought to the altar. Who and what he was gave virtue to all that he accomplished. The difference between the religions of the world and Christianity is that in the former, man provides a sacrifice for his god, but in the latter God provides a sacrifice for man. God was the source of Calvary's love. Had he not so loved the world, there would have been no reconciliation. Jesus in no way mollified the wrath of God— he bore its limit on our behalf. There is an arrestive phrase in the offering up of Isaac. When Abraham had prepared the altar, Isaac asked, "Where is the lamb for a burnt offering?" and his father replied, "My son, God will provide *himself* a lamb" (Gen. 22:7, 8). God, in the Person of his Son, did provide *himself* as the burnt offering. Paul uses the pregnant phrase, "Feed the church of God, which he (God) hath purchased with his own blood" (Acts 20:28). The blood shed at the Cross, then, was not merely the blood of Mary's child, but of God's Son. Both God and man died, for Jesus was the God-Man, and his sacrifice is eternally efficacious for in it deity was united with humanity. The blood has transcendent power owing to its unique character as the blood of the Lord Jesus Christ, God's Son.

THE LOAD: "Which beareth away the sin of the world"

In ancient times the blood of bulls and goats secured an outward religious position for the offerer, but could not save him as a sinner. Yet it was accepted in prospect of the virtue of the blood to be shed when God provided a perfect Sacrifice for sin. The death of *the* Lamb operates in the sphere of the spiritual. It is inward, bringing the sinner nigh unto God and securing his acceptance by him.

Its Banishment: "Beareth away"

The word for "beareth" implies a lifting up and carrying away. What love! Jesus took up the accursed load of the world's sin, made it his own, and which, because of it was such a mountain of iniquity caused God to turn his face away from its bearer. The scapegoat offered as a sin-offering bore the load into the banished land of forgetfulness (Lev. 16:8–10). In becoming our sin offering Jesus took up the burden of sin, too heavy for us to carry, and bore it away into oblivion. "Your sins and iniquities will I remember no more."

Its Character: "The sin"

The gospel verse does not say sins but *sin*—not the fruit but the root. Emphasis is on the article *the*. What do you feel *the* sin is? Doubtless personal estimation of same will differ according to one's outlook and experience. Some would say drunkenness, others gambling, still others, immorality, and so on; and the effort is made to fight against the separate sins of the world. Many reformers, brave in the attempt, have tried to kill this sin and the other, but failed. Streams and fruit were dealt with but not the fountain, or root. But when Jesus died it was for sin, and his removal of it is both inward and radical. *The* sin consists in omitting God from the life, forgetting and ignoring him, breaking his commands and incurring his judgment thereby. But the death and blood of the Redeemer is the diamond set in the golden ring of the gospel, for by them we are delivered from *sin.*

Its Enormity: "The world"

The sin of the world, and a world of sin, what a burden to fall upon the holy heart of the Lamb! The phrase, "the sin of the world," refers to the weight and extent of sin, as well as its nature and character. Christ gave himself for our sin—and sins—that he might deliver us from "this present evil world." He died to free us from its *spirit,* by which we are influenced in a state of nature, from the *love* of the world, which is enmity with God. He died to free us from seeking *satisfaction* in the world, which is idolatry, from the *doom* of the world, which is eternal woe. Can we say that we are dead to the sin of the world because of our fellowship with him in death?

It would have been bad enough for him as the Holy One to bear our sin; but such was his love and pity that he bore the massive load of the world's sin. Think of the sin of one life—in early days after the consciousness of right and wrong, in youth, manhood, old age, and then multiply such by all the millions who have lived, are living, and will yet live, and then realize, if you can, the awful load he bore as the Substitute for sinners. Well might we *Behold,* for nothing can wash away our sin but the precious blood he shed. It is useless waiting, trying to understand the Atonement—we must believe the fact. We do not wait to understand electricity before using it. We simply press the switch and we have light and power. In salvation, the possible becomes actual as we look and believe, and as soon as we do we are cleansed from the guilt and power of sin—the double cure the slain Lamb provides.

1. *The Guilt.* Sin on the conscience can become a terrible load, and men try in all ways to get rid of it. One thing conscience cannot do, it cannot forgive. It can condemn, accuse, point out our wrongdoing, but it cannot remove the sin of which it ever reminds us. When forgiven by divine grace, our sin may remain as a fact of history, as its results also do, but it no longer accuses. This is why we sing:

> I take, O Cross, thy shadow
> For my abiding-place;
> I ask no other sunshine than
> The sunshine of His face;
> Content to let the world go by,
> To know no gain or loss,
> My sinful self my only shame,
> My glory all the Cross.
> *Elizabeth C. Clephane*

2. *The Power.* A full deliverance is only ours when we are emancipated, not only from the guilt of sin, but from its power. "He breaks the power of cancelled sin." The sin-bound, devil-possessed soul must look by faith to the Lamb who loved him and died to loose him from the chains binding him. There is no other way whereby his burdened heart and life can be mantled with victory. The burden of sin is removed, as he who died for sin is received by a saving faith.

> Dear dying Lamb! Thy precious blood
> Shall never lose its power,
> Till all the ransomed church of God
> Be saved to sin no more.
> *William Cowper*

Unto him that loved us, and washed us from our sins in his own blood (Rev. 1:5).

13 /

The Doxology of the Redeemed

In the closing words of Christ on earth, in the preaching of *The Acts,* the appeals of the *Epistles,* and the unfolding in *The Revelation,* the prominent, or eclipsing topic is that of redemption through the death of the Cross. In fact, the New Testament knows no other gospel save the one scorned today, namely, that Christ died for the ungodly. A noble army of men and women have hazarded their lives, at home and abroad, for Christ, being actuated by the passion of the Cross. Millions on earth and in glory who have experienced pardon, peace, and purity, all with united breath—

> Ascribe their victory to the Lamb,
> Their triumph to His death.
> *Author Unknown*

This is why we make no apology in continuing to proclaim the blessed theme of the shed blood of the world's Redeemer. Thus, in this meditation we are to discover how that precious blood operates as a cleansing factor in the lives of sinners— a class to which we all belong.

CLEANSES BY REVEALING THE TRUE NATURE OF SIN

Sin is the most evident and dreadful fact of life. As Dr. E. B. Pusey put it, "The sun never sets on sin." How true! Because of our relationship to our first parents we are born with a sinning nature and an inborn love of evil. As we enter into life we fall under the power of sin, as it comes to us clothed with light and masked beauty, and radiant with charms. But it need not keep its dominion over us, if we always see behind it the features of the devil, hellish parent of all sin. It is only after we have sinned that we realize how deluded we have been, and the mask of an angel of light is torn off when we discover how hideous a thing sin is, in the sight of a thrice holy God. When we are sorely tempted, a look at Christ's marred face will save us from committal. To see the leering eyes of the Tempter as he seeks to seduce, and then turn to his glorious Victor, prevents temptation becoming sin.

Mark how the supreme sacrifice of the Cross exposes the particular sin of those beneath its shadow. The dastardly betrayal of Jesus by Judas is made more despicable, horrible, and callous in the pure white light of the Cross.

Gross and debauched Herod stands revealed in all his nakedness in the sight of the crucified Savior whom he helped to murder.

The cowardly spite of Pilate, who did not have the courage of his inner convictions, is made more visible alongside the Cross he was responsible for erecting.

Focus the awful light of Calvary upon the life you live and experience how you are able to recoil from things you presently love that are alien to the will of God. Bad temper, petty pride, empty vanity, worldliness, and prayerlessness evoke shame when lifted up to the Cross. We can never visit Golgotha without finding some fresh aspect of sin's diabolical nature. If we have doubt about anything, the Cross is the acid test.

A small group of students decided to travel through Switzerland. They were eager to get away from godly homes where life was too rigid and narrow for them. In their travels they came to a rudely shaped cross by the wayside, at the foot of which lay a few cheap offerings placed there by the poor peasants near by. At the sight of the rude cross, silence fell upon the youths, and the full impact of the thoughts of their hearts overtook them. They saw their own heartlessness and sinfulness. Making confession there they returned home, cleansed by the blood of Jesus. This is the only way by which we can be freed from the guilt of sin. How glorious and divine to know that we can be purged from all sin, saved from wrath, and made the righteousness of God in him who shed his ruby blood on the Cross.

What must be kept in mind as we deal with the unconverted, is that it is altogether the wrong approach to ask them to surrender their glittering toys, questionable habits, and much loved pleasures. This negative appeal is contrary to the gospel plan which is not "give up" but "take." In a positive way, we must present God's method of salvation, namely, redemption by the blood of Jesus and regeneration by the Spirit. Once a sinner bows before him whose scarred and bleeding form made deliverance from sin possible, his chains fall off, and he is loosed from his sin. The vain things that charmed him most are quickly surrendered to his blood.

This was the experience of the one penning these lines. Well over seventy years ago my life was diverted from its emptiness, frivolity, and uncleanness into a purer, nobler channel. I was a stagestruck youth, and my eyes gazed upon the sights that dazzle young hearts in theatres and music halls. But one night in a gospel meeting my vision was directed to the greatest drama ever acted on the world's stage—the bitter death of God's fairest and best. And the sight of him hanging on a tree for *me* won my young heart, and I became one of the vast company no man can number, washed in the blood of the Lamb. When Christ is received by faith as a personal Savior, our sins and follies fall as dead leaves from a tree.

CLEANSES BY UNFOLDING THE LOVE OF GOD

Judas went out from the Supper, where he gazed upon the face of sorrow and heard the final appeal of love. Then he made his fatal bargain. Many a child brought up in a godly home, under the influence of a father's prayers and a mother's sanctity, has yet passed out into the haunts of sin. It is possible for the highest and most beautiful life not to touch other hearts impelling them to live a purer life. But the mightier power compelling us to follow the light is the longsuffering love of God, a love no waters can quench. Nothing so shames us for our sin and unfaithfulness, inspiring us to live at our best, like the sacrificial love of God. When we look up at the Cross and see this love revealed in his only begotten Son as he hangs there, torn and bleeding for our sakes, then there passes through our hearts a new penitence, deep confession, full surrender, issuing in a life satisfying to Jesus for the travail of his soul.

A classic illustration of this divine love to cleanse from sin is found in the biography of Captain Hedley Vicars, one-time British officer in the Indian Army. As a youth he was blameless and amiable. He came early under religious influences, which became part of him. Although religious, he was still not saved. But one day the truth of the love of God revealed at Calvary flashed upon his heart, and he came to experience cleansing by the blood. Here is the account of that transformation as given by his biographer:

"It was in the month of November, 1851, that, whilst

awaiting the return of a brother officer to his rooms, he idly turned over the leaves of a Bible which lay on the table. The words caught his eye, 'The blood of Jesus Christ, God's Son, cleanseth from all sin.' Closing the Book, he said, 'If this be true for me, henceforth I will live by the grace of God, as a man should live who has been washed in the blood of the Lamb. The past, then, is blotted out. What I have to do is to go forward. I cannot return to the sins from which my Saviour has cleansed me in His own blood.' "

The heart of the gospel is that no matter how much one has sinned, God still loves the sinner and yearns to cleanse him from his sin. God is love. The Cross reveals it, the Scriptures proclaim it, the Spirit declares it, and it is for the sinner to believe it and rest in the fact of it.

Cleanses by Removing Our Iniquities

What a priceless jewel of divine revelation this is: "The blood of Jesus Christ . . . cleanseth us from *all* sin." (1 John 1:7). Cleansed, delivered from the shackles of sin, not by our own self-effort, self-righteousness, good deeds, churchgoing, and religious acts, but solely by the blood of Jesus the Mediator, whose blood "speaketh better things than that of Abel" (Heb. 12:24). No matter if one is without guilt like Nathanael, he must die without hope unless he is sheltered by the out-poured blood. On his dying bed an aged minister asked one near by, "Bring me the Bible." Putting his finger on the verse, "The blood of Jesus Christ . . . cleanseth us from all sin," he said, "I die in hope of this blessed verse." It was not his good life, or fifty years of preaching, but absolute dependence upon the blood that bore the faithful pastor over the dark waters of death.

1. *Unceasing Virtue.* It will be noticed that John uses the present tense, *cleanseth* (1 John 1:7). While, at conver-

sion, there is an initial, definite cleansing, the action is repeated, and is continuous, for we are ever in need of the crimson tide, and will be until we are saved to sin no more. Some may cherish the blindest of all delusions, that they are already perfect and have no need of further cleansing. But many of us are only too conscious of the subtle attractions of the old nature, to believe that we can do without the unceasing virtue of the blood that flowed from the Redeemer's veins. If we would walk in undisturbed peace of heart, we must bring every sin, no matter how small, to the blood the moment we are conscious of the need for cleansing. We have need to see greater depths of sin in our nature, and greater depths of grace and cleansing in him who died for our sins.

2. *Unlimited Victory.* Do you not love the *all* in this most marvelous verse? The blood cleanseth, not from some, but *all* kinds and degrees of sin. We may give different names to such, but God knows only one name—*sin.* If we could marshall all the sins committed, we would shriek with horror and close our eyes in disgust. There are sins against God and man, sins against the Sabbath and the sacraments, sins against the body and soul, light and knowledge and conscience, against the Bible and the church, against dear ones and friends. But the glorious truth is that no sin is too terrible for the blood to cleanse, no matter how black, ugly, horrible or selfish it may be.

The blood that flowed from Calvary contains sufficient efficacy to wash away every stain of any sinner the world over if only he will believe the truth. It is only the blood of Jesus who died in our room and stead that cleanses, and which has perpetual virtue and victory because of who he was. If he died only as a martyr for some truth he believed, then his blood has no more value than the blood which faithful Stephen shed.

No, what sins we have been guilty of, whether of a gross

nature, or the finer sins of pride and self-righteousness, all we can do is to bring the terrible load to the Cross, the blood of which can snap the strongest fetter hell ever forged. "His blood can make the vilest clean, his blood avails for me."

The story is told of two simple souls who seldom read a book, but who gained possession of a Bible, which they read with great zest. The Holy Spirit brought home to their minds the truth of God's free salvation through the death of the Savior. "Wife," the husband exclaimed, "if this book is true, we are lost." But as they read on, the blessed truth of cleansing and deliverance for all sin by the blood was fully revealed to them, and the man cried, "Wife, if this book is true, we can be saved." And saved they were.

Yes, apart from Christ, man is lost, helpless, and hopeless. But because God loves him and gave his Son to die as the sinner's substitute, he can be freed from his sin, and from the devil responsible for all sin—if he comes without one plea, save that the blood of Jesus was shed for him. Then, once saved, he, too, can join in the doxology of the redeemed.

It behoved Christ to suffer. . . . Ye are witnesses of these things (Luke 24:46, 48).

14 /

Who Saw Him Die?

How haunting is the refrain of the negro spiritual, "Were you there when they crucified my Lord?" Many witnessed that grim spectacle, and we are to identify the beholders of those three crosses at Calvary, particularly the middle Cross on which our Lord was crucified.

What a mixed, diverse crowd formed the Calvary tableau! Friend and foe alike saw him die, and his death impressed its varying effect upon those who gazed at his agony, for the Cross distinguishes man from man and is the acid estimate of character, as well as the test of personal attitude toward truth.

The world has its way of dividing men into different classes, rich or poor, learned or ignorant, fortunate or unfortunate, but God's way of separating man is by his Son's Cross, which is the judgment of this world (John 12:31). As every man comes into sight of the Cross, he finds himself judged there, and sees himself as God sees him.

While we were not there when they crucified our Lord, the witnesses of that terrible scene were representative of people today, for around the Cross the whole human family is gathered, every man of every race, and any race of men, and they are judged beneath its shadow. As we shall see, the Cross reveals the best—and the worst—in human nature.

> I see the crowd in Pilate's hall,
> I mark their wrathful mien.
> Their shouts of "Crucify!" appall,
> With blasphemy between.
> But of that shouting multitude,
> I feel that I am one.
> *Horatius Bonar*

Among the friends and foes who were present at Golgotha and saw him die, the Gospels name the following:

Simon of Cyrene was there!

It would be interesting to know why out of the whole crowd hurrying to the place of crucifixion the centurion chose this man from North Africa to take up the Cross on which Jesus was to die, and bear it after him (Luke 23:26). Was he chosen because he possessed good, broad shoulders, or was it because he was suspected a secret disciple? Tradition has it that after carrying the Cross, and seeing Jesus die on it, Simon became an avowed Christian. Evidently his two sons, Alexander and Rufus, were well-known to the church when Mark came to write his Gospel (15:21).

If Simon was a disciple, then he was qualified to become a sharer of his Master's humiliation, for only those who are his own can take up the cross and follow him. How striking is the phrase, "On him they laid the cross" (Luke 23:26). In after days, what pride would be his as he recounted the story of Via Dolorosa, and how he bore the Cross all the way, and watched Jesus die on it.

Artists have depicted Simon carrying the heavy end of the Cross, and Jesus with the lightest end on his shoulder. But Scripture says that Simon bore it *after* Jesus, which implies that Jesus was ahead of the bearer. After being scourged by Pilate, the back and shoulders of Jesus would be too raw and lacerated to bear the lightest load (Luke 23:22). Doubtless, as Simon watched the Savior die on the gibbet he had borne to the spot where it was erected, he sighed and wished he was able to relieve him of his agony. That Cross had been on his back, but now the back of Jesus was on it, sore and bleeding, after he had given it to the smiters (Isa. 50:6).

Barabbas was there!

Curiosity alone would constrain this murderer to travel with the other sightseers, to catch a glimpse of the Man who was to die on the Cross. It was the one on which he should have justly died for his crimes. Barabbas, convicted and condemned for insurrection and killings, waited, along with the two thieves, for crucifixion. He should have paid the penalty on that middle cross, but weak Pilate surrendered Jesus as his substitute. Thus, Barabbas was the first person to be saved from death through the death of the sinner's Substitute. Doubtless, if he saw him die, gazing up at his marred face, he would say, "He died in my room and stead." It is to be hoped that he found peace through believing. The glory of the gospel is that Jesus endured death, not only that which Barabbas should have suffered, but death for every man (Heb. 2:9).

Nicodemus was there!

This highly educated and deeply religious Jewish teacher is always described as the one who came to Jesus "by night" (John 3:1, 2; 7:50; 19:39). What happened after that first memorable occasion when Jesus and he met, we are not told. He listened intently to the conversation about regeneration and asked Jesus questions. Nicodemus was a sincere inquirer, and it would seem that he came to experience what it was to be born again, but remained a secret disciple. When division arose because of Jesus' teaching, he spoke up in his defense, but his plea was unavailing. Then he must have been at the Cross when Jesus died for he assisted in his burial and indicated thereby that he was no longer a secret disciple. As soon as he knew the leading members of the Council had decided upon the death of Jesus, he secured the necessary spices to perfume his body, and linen clothes to cover it. The sight of Calvary brought him out into the open and led him to publicly identify himself with One he had inwardly reverenced. Mary gave her costly spices to Jesus while he was alive and could appreciate them— Nicodemus kept his myrrh and aloes for the death of Jesus. Alas, however, no corpse can appreciate rich perfumes. Why save all our flowers until our friends die? Why not let them enjoy their fragrance while they live?

The daughters of Jerusalem were there!

Among those swelling the crowd as Jesus painfully trod the Calvary road were these women of mercy, who were not animated by any sentiment beyond pity as they watched the holy Sufferer sinking beneath his load. They were professional weepers who lamented and bewailed each victim forcibly led to Golgotha. Sincere and commendable though their tears were, they were simply brought on by the plight of this Son of some sorrowing mother. Had theirs not been mere emotion, Jesus would not have responded to their lamentation with the sad severity he did when he said, "Weep not for me, but weep for yourselves, and for your children" (Luke 23:28). Save your tears, he implied, for you will have need to shed them over your coming sorrows. Is it not true to say that there are many like those compassionate daughters of Jerusalem who are emotionally moved when they read or hear about the sufferings of Christ, but beyond admiration for his amazing patience under affliction, their hearts do not travel? He does not want our tears, but our trust—not our sobs, but our full surrender to his claims—not our sympathy but our submission to his will.

The three Marys were there!

The closest relatives and friends were silent witnesses that dark day, for they, too, saw him die. There was Mary, his dear mother, and his brothers and sisters if these are included in "all his acquaintances," who saw the conspicuous member of the Nazareth home die. What agony must have been Mary's as she beheld the Son of her womb hanging on that Cross! Hers was the first face he saw when he was born in Bethlehem. Now it was the last, as he tenderly committed her to John's care.

Then there was the other Mary, the sister of Mary, his mother, and as the Lord's aunt, unutterable agony was also hers as she watched her illustrious Nephew die. Sorrow has a binding influence seen in the way these relatives kept together until the member of the family on the Cross was severed from human ties.

As for Mary Magdalene, where else would she be but at the place of crucifixion to see him die to whom she owed so much? Had Jesus not saved her from something worse than death when he cast out her seven demons and restored her reason and self-respect? So she, too, stood by the Cross that the image of that marred face might be stamped upon her heart. It is profitable to observe that although the soldiers *sat* at the foot of the Cross, these heartstricken women *stood* by it. They were not prostrate on the ground, but like sentinels stood on guard. No woman had a hand in his death, and thus, courageously, "having done all to stand," they must have comforted the dying Savior by their posture.

The disciples were there!

Speaking for all the Apostles, Peter said of Jesus slain and hanged upon a tree, "We are witnesses of these things" (Acts 5:32). When the servants of the high priest came to take Jesus, seeing their swords and staves, his disciples forsook him and fled. True, Peter acted somewhat hastily in the defense of his Master, and he had to repair the damage done. One wonders what their feelings were like when after having forsaken him, they saw him die. While John is the only apostle mentioned as standing by the Cross, all the others must have been near by, for one of the qualifications for apostleship was that of witnessing the death and resurrection of Jesus. Thus, the other eleven saw him crucified—including Matthias, who was chosen in the place of Judas (Acts 1:13, 22, 26; 5:32). The Epistles of Peter, John, James, and Jude, reveal the impact of the Cross upon their hearts and minds.

As Peter, possibly on the fringe of the crowd listening to their jeers and jibes, watched Jesus die, tears of penitence must have been his, for he had vowed to go to death with him, and die the same kind of death—which he later did. Legend tells us that the apostle felt so unworthy to die in the same way as his Lord that he begged his crucifiers to crucify him upside down. This was the disciple who could write of being redeemed by "the precious blood of Christ, as of a lamb without blemish and without spot" (1 Peter 1:19).

The Centurion was there!

The *centurion,* a term related to "century," was an officer in the Roman army who commanded a company of 100 soldiers. The centurion at Calvary was the one detailed to carry out the grim task of crucifying the victims, and his

share in the death shows how both Jew and Gentile were
united in the dastardly action of killing the Son of God.
But somehow, although he had crucified an untold number
of men condemned to die in such fashion, there was something totally different about the Man dying on that middle
Cross. As the earthquake rocked the city the moment Jesus
died, smitten with fear, the centurion felt there had been
a miscarriage of justice in the death of such a Godlike Man.
So he cried, "Truly this was the Son of God" (Matt. 27:54).
It may be that as the centurion surveyed the wondrous Cross
on which the Prince of Glory died, he came to experience
his saving power.

The soldiers were there!

These rough pagans of the Roman army, under the command of the centurion, accustomed to driving the nails
through the hands and feet of the victims, had no sympathy
for anguish and suffering. A brutal insensitivity was theirs.
Because of their callous hearts they could kill without turning a hair. As they sat down to watch him die they gambled
for the clothes they had stripped from Jesus (Matt. 27:36).
What a contrast this affords! While the highest Love was
on the Cross praying, at its foot deepest hate was indifferent.
Being dead was not enough for these brutal crucifiers, for
one of them pierced the side of Jesus. Alas! even today
there are those who because of the hardness of heart and
intensity of engrossment in earthly things, reject Christ with
scarcely a thought. To them, it is nothing as they pass by
his Cross.

The two thieves were there!

All three, hanging on their respective crosses, saw each
other die. Although they were dying the same death, and
enduring the same terrible anguish, there was this marked

difference between them: The two thieves were dying for
their own sin, but Jesus, the sinless One, was dying for
the sin of others. While both thieves at the outset reviled
Jesus, one of them repented and begged for mercy. As
Browning expressed it, "The last kind word Christ spoke
was to a thief." As William Cowper wrote:

> "The dying thief rejoiced to see
> That fountain in his day. . . ."

—and so he entered paradise, the first trophy of the efficacious Redeemer's blood. The other thief died as he had
lived, without God and without hope. The Cross divides:
one thief went to paradise, the other to perdition. "One
was saved that none might despair, but only one that none
might presume."

The religious leaders were there!

The priests, scribes, and elders, forming the Sanhedrin
who had constantly plotted to kill Jesus during his ministry,
saw him and gloated over his death (Matt. 27:20, 42; Luke
23:35). These religious leaders *derided* him—a word meaning "the curled lip, and distended nostril of scorn." With
hate in their eyes they saw him die. They had cried at his
trial, "Away with him, crucify him," and now, as he died,
they mocked him with taunts like: "He saved others, himself
he cannot save"; "Let him come down from the cross, and
we will believe him." They wanted religion but not a Redeemer, a Messiah without a Cross. Many of them, however,
were transformed by the manifestation of divine power in
the earthquake and the resurrection of the dead, for we
read that a "great company of priests were obedient to the
faith" (Acts 6:7). In our century we have those who are
religious before men, but who have no room for the Man
who died, either in their religion or inner experience.

The universe was there!

How could Christ's love and death sound the unfathomable depths and embrace unspeakable agonies—and the universe he had brought into being not hasten to his aid? The firmament was his handiwork, and thus Nature hurried to turn midday into midnight to hide the shame heaped upon her Creator, and cover his nakedness with a garment of black (Matt. 27:45). Godless eyes would look at him and stare (Ps. 22:17), and so darkness covered the earth so that his bleeding and naked body could not be seen (Luke 23:44, 45). Isaac Watts has the stanza:

> Well might the sun in darkness hide,
>   And shut his glories in,
> When God, the mighty Maker, died
>   For man the creature's sin.

In addition to the noonday darkness, we have the mysterious rending of the temple veil, the earthquake resulting in the resurrection of the dead, as further evidence of Nature's interest in the One the godless were crucifying as a felon on a wooden gibbet.

God was there!

While the fourth cry from the Cross might suggest that God was not there to see his Son die, yet as the Omniscient One he witnessed all that transpired at Calvary. Had God not planned the Cross when he told Satan that the seed of a woman would bruise his head, even though he would bruise the heel of the Victor (Gen. 3:15)? While God, *as God,* could not look upon the sin of the world his Son was bearing, yet in the darkness he was near. The shadow of forsakenness soon passed, and in his last conscious moments, Jesus knew his Father had not left him alone, hence the final cry, "Father, into thy hands I commend my spirit" (Luke 23:46). What a victorious way to die! May our end be like his, committing ourselves to our heavenly Father's care.

The Holy Spirit was there!

In declaring that the apostles were witnesses of the death and resurrection of Jesus, Peter went on to use the most pertinent phrase, "So also was the Holy Spirit" (Acts 5:32). Later on, Peter came to write that the Spirit "testified beforehand the sufferings of Christ," and saw him die (1 Peter 1:11). Before he died, Jesus had named the Spirit as the *Comforter,* and we can imagine how he was present upholding, consoling, and whispering to the dying One in the hours of his travail. He was not only a divine witness of his sufferings, but also the One who imparted his sweet, soothing influences.

You were there!

The negro spiritual asks the question, "Were you there when they crucified my Lord?" Yes, we were there in a representative sense, for he was dying for your sins and mine. While we were not actually present, as others were, to watch him die, yet he had us in mind when he climbed those bloody slopes for he died in our place. With Paul each of us can say, he "gave himself for me" (Gal. 2:20). In his marred countenance, and nail-pierced hands and feet, I read the guarantee of my salvation. His blood-shedding and redeeming grace were for me, and I am crowned with honor and glory if I have the assurance that I am one of the vast multitude washed by the blood of the Lamb.

In his essay on *The Trial of Jesus,* John Masefield gives us a semihistorical, semi-imaginative, but withal a reverent treatment of the theme. At one point in the story Masefield relates a conversation between Pilate's wife and the centurion who had charge of the crucifixion. Procula says to Longinus, "Do you think He is dead?" To which Longinus replies, "No, lady, I don't." "Then where is He?" ask Pilate's wife.

"Where is He?" exclaimed the centurion, *"Let loose in the world where neither Roman nor Jew can stop His truth."*

Alive forevermore, he is let loose in a world in which none can stop him! Men crucified him to silence him, but he rose again from the grave, and since then he has marched triumphantly through the centuries reaping a glorious harvest of those redeemed by his blood, and the devil and all hell cannot impede his continuing victories, the fruit of his soul-travail.

> Only one Cross!
> And to that Cross He leadeth all His own:
> They gather round it, and its healing falls
> Upon each sinful one.
> *Author Unknown*

15 /

His Broken Body

How utterly dependent we are upon the Holy Spirit who witnessed the last poignant hours of the Redeemer, for an understanding of all he willingly endured as the Man of Sorrows! With our finite minds it is impossible for us to grasp the inner significance of all He suffered on our behalf. It would appear as if his grief was fourfold in nature.

There were his material sufferings, seen in the lack of many things contributing to his mortal comfort, such as money, sleep, nowhere to lay his head, and the pure joys of life.

There were his mental afflictions—those indescribable inward tortures often worse to endure than outward pain. His cry of God-forsakenness revealed anguish of mind.

There were his spiritual sorrows, leading him to confess, "My soul is exceeding sorrowful, even unto death" (Matt. 26:38). The veil is drawn over these for none of the ransomed can ever know what their dear Lord passed through to redeem them.

There were his physical agonies which Paul implies in

Christ's body being "broken for you." It is not morbid to dwell on these outward sufferings. The realization of their grim nature enables us to grasp, in some measure, the infinite cost of our salvation.

When Jesus took the bread and broke it, he declared it to be a fitting emblem of his body about to be bruised and broken for the sin of the world. Those who affirm that when we partake of the bread and wine at the Lord's Table we actually eat his flesh and drink his blood greatly err, for the elements are only the symbols he chose of himself, as the Bread of Life, crushed and broken on our behalf. As "the life of the flesh is in the blood," in the outpoured wine, he illustrated the sacrifice of his life for others. As *seven* is the number of perfection, we have therein a glimpse of the limit of physical agonies Jesus experienced as he died for our sake:

1. *His Face Was Marred:* "His visage was so marred more than any man" (Isa. 52:14).

The literal rendering is more terrible, implying that his face was battered beyond human recognition. The prophet describes the brutalities heaped upon his fair and beautiful countenance until it was hardly distinguishable as the face of a man. Isaiah also depicts this torture in the phrases, "I gave my back to the smiters, and my cheeks to them that plucked off the hair: I hid not my face from shame and spitting. . . . I set my face like a flint" (50:6). Matthew quotes this prophecy and adds, "others smote him with the palms of their hands" (27:67). Being fairer than the children of men, Jesus must have had a "human face divine," and therefore one of surpassing beauty, charm, and loveliness. There must have been real continual comfort in that Face. We are living in an age in which colossal sums are spent in the creation of false facial beauty and the cosmetics used must be harmful to the skin. Jesus, however, had an appealing attractiveness of face, God-created, yet marred, destroyed by those who had no sense of beauty they could desire.

Sometimes God permits the disfigurement of natural facial good looks, and although it is hard for the flesh to part with same, this was the way the Master went. When only twenty-two years of age, Madam Guyon had her beautiful face smitten during a scourge of smallpox. As she lay in bed suffering from the total deprivation of the beauty that had been a snare to her pride, she experienced a joy unspeakable. What others lamented over, she now rejoiced at, and as soon as she was able and well again, she went out into the streets where she used to exalt her lovely face and showed her horrible scars. The Savior did not hide his face from shame, spitting, and smiting, for in spite of the brutalities awaiting him, he set his face as a flint. With a voice vibrating with heavenly music, he could sing, "I delight to do thy will, O my God" (Ps. 40:8), even though he knew that part of that will meant the disfigurement of his face which radiated love and compassion. What a gruesome sight that face must have been at Calvary, all blood-spattered after the smiting and the plucking of hair it had received! Yet grossly disfigured it carried a smile as it was turned to the repentant dying thief. Our blessed hope is expressed by John, "They shall see his face," and when we come to gaze upon his countenance, it will be perfectly beautiful, shining eternally as the sun. And, what a privilege will be ours when we see him as he now is, for "we shall be like him" (1 John 3:2).

2. *His Brow Was Scarred:* "When they had plaited a crown of thorns, they put it upon his head" (Matt. 27:29).

The *brow* represents something conspicuous and prominent. Thus we speak of the "brow" of a hill because of its protrusion. Byron could write of one, "Time writes no wrinkle on thine azure brow," indicating that this part of the head is the seat of wisdom and intelligence. The shape of the brow often reveals the mentality of its possessor. At the Cross, Christ's brow was pierced by many a thorn—emblem of the curse occasioned by sin as Eden proves. The thorn-crowned brow is also representative of the fact of human wisdom, no matter how greatly cursed by sin. Man's wisdom is foolishness to God and can only be acceptable to him when fleshly knowledge is crucified. We have no wisdom of our own commendable to God. This is why he made Christ to be our Wisdom. Man may love the wisdom of this world, but as this is not his wisdom, it must go. A further thought is that by his scarred and bleeding brow, Jesus brought all the powers of the mind, and so, having a redeemed mind we sing:

> Take my intellect, and use
> Every power as Thou shalt choose.
> *Frances Ridley Havergal*

Unless the brow bears the imprint of the thorns its product will be of little use to him whose brow was crowned with thorns.

3. *His Back Was Lacerated:* "I gave my back to the smiters" (Isa. 50:6).

"He (Pilate) . . . scourged Jesus" (Matt. 27:26). The Roman form of punishment indicated by such smiting and scourging involved the hands being tied to a pillar, the back bared and bent to receive the lashes of knotted thongs of leather. The English *cat,* or birch used to punish prisoners, was a similar form of penalty. The pain and agony of such stripes must be excruciating, yet Jesus willingly received the full smiting, and, says Isaiah, "with his stripes we are healed" (53:5). It was no wonder that Jesus fell as he tried to carry the heavy cross. With his back lacerated and bleeding, bringing intense pain, he was not able to shoulder the burden. The marvel is that such suffering was voluntary, for the prophecy says, "I *gave* my back to the smiters." Willingly, Jesus submitted to the lashes. He offered himself to the cruel punishment that should have been ours. What wonderful condescension! He was not forced to bare his sacred body to receive the scourging, but he actually assisted the smiters in their gruesome task; and all for love of those who had turned their backs on him. What marvelous, vicarious suffering!

4. *His Side Was Pierced:* "One of the soldiers with a spear pierced his side, and forthwith came there out blood and water" (John 19:34).

It is a medical fact that the combination of blood and water is an evidence of a torn, pierced, or broken heart. Although punctured by the soldier's spear, it was already a broken heart caused by the depth of his anguish and grief, and the intolerable load of the world's sin. Not only was his body broken, his heart was also torn. Thus he was doubly broken because of our sin—outwardly, the body: inwardly, the heart. The twofold stream of blood and water can typify Calvary and Pentecost, and we have need of both, the blood of the Redeemer to cleanse us from the guilt of sin, and the Holy Spirit—likened unto water—to deliver us from the government of sin. So we sing with Augustus Montague Toplady:

> Rock of Ages, cleft for me,
> Let me hide myself in Thee;
> Let the water and the blood,
> From Thy riven side which flowed,
> Be of sin the double cure,
> Cleanse me from its guilt and power.

There is this deeper truth, however, in the punctured heart of Jesus. By such, he brought the power of our heart's love and affection, which means we must pour at his feet Love's treasure store. We can no longer love the world that broke his loving heart, or suffer our affection to stream out to carnal pleasures that helped to crucify him who loved not the world, nor the things in it alien to his will.

5. *His Hands Were Nailed:* "They pierced my hands"; "The print of the nails"; "He shewed them his hands" (Ps. 22:16; John 20:25; Luke 24:40).

As we gaze at those nailed, pierced hands we marvel at their added charm and power, and life-giving, vivifying influence. The Jews thought they had ended the power of those blessed hands when they nailed them to a tree. Fools! they only added to their virtue. Great might and majesty are seen in the way those pierced palms have conquered souls all down the ages. The peace of the world is to come from the hands that still bear the marks of the nails:

> And those Hands hold,
> Though pierced with nails
> They hold on still,
> Through power and pain.
> And they shall hold
> Till Satan falls
> And love comes to its own to reign.
> *Author Unknown*

We can fully appreciate the hesitancy of Thomas over the acceptance of the testimony of the other disciples who came to him and said, "We have seen the Lord!" The reply of Thomas was explicit:

"Except I shall see in his hands the print of the nails . . . I will not believe" (John 20:25).

The moment he saw the insignia of his suffering, he said, "My Lord, and my God." To him no person could claim to be his Lord, unless he bore the wound prints of the Cross. Would that the same evidence was sought in these times when many in religious circles want a Christ without the print of the nails. They exalt him as the Christ of Galilee, magnificent teacher and social reformer, but they will not own him as the Christ of Golgotha, whose "rich wounds are still visible above." We accept no Christ who does not bear the imprint of nails and a riven side. With those torn hands, he bought our hands with all their wonderful power. Do our hands bear the marks of the nails? Crucified hands know instinctively what to accept or refuse. They cannot engage in anything dishonest, shady, or illegitimate. They cannot handle things tainted by sin. With Frances Ridley Havergal let us sing:

> Take my hands, and let them move
> At the impulse of Thy love.

6. *His feet were torn:* "They pierced . . . my feet"; "He shewed . . . them his feet"; "How beautiful . . . are the feet of him that bringeth good tidings" (Ps. 22:16; Luke 24:40; Isa. 52:7).

As the heaven-sent messenger, Jesus had beautiful feet as he traveled here and there preaching and teaching, and performing his miraculous works. Often weary and dust-laden when his feet would carry him no further, he would have to rest, as he did when he met the woman at the well. As he rested his tired feet, he dealt with a sin-crushed heart using lovely tact and tenderness. But the feet, ever active on errands of mercy, were nailed fast to the tree, as if man had the power to curb their journeys to a world in need. Yet crucified feet walk this earth, for the nailing of them to a Cross only added to their progress. Any place those feet now stand on is made glorious. Isaac Watts sum-

marizes for us the spiritual implication of that wondrous
Cross on which Christ's body was broken:

> See from His head, His hands, His feet,
>   Sorrow and love flow mingled down;
> Did e'er such love and sorrow meet,
>   Or thorns compose so rich a crown?

Those torn, bleeding feet teach us to be ever ready to run
his errands, to be "swift and beautiful" for him. If our feet
bear the Calvary marks, they will not take us into places,
or into company, where he is dishonored and despised. Crucified feet are careful how they walk, and where they should
travel.

7. *His whole body was humiliated:* "His visage was so marred
more than any man"; "I may tell all my bones: they look
and stare at me" (Isa. 52:14; Ps. 22:17; cp. Matt. 27:35,
36).

Before placing Jesus upon the Cross, the soldiers stripped
him naked and gambled for his garments and vesture. Thus
his pure, holy body, unclothed, was exposed to the unholy
gaze of the mob who had demanded his crucifixion. All
sense of dignity, propriety, and decency were outraged in
this foul act of humiliation, when he was exhibited almost
nude for the godless to gape at with their mouths, as they
stared at all his bones. What base treatment for the One
who had provided the first inhabitants of earth with clothing
to cover their nakedness! No wonder Nature hurried to hide
her Lord with a garment of darkness, as "His dying crimson,
like a robe, Spread o'er His body on the tree."

The symbolic aspect of this exposure is not far to seek.
He was there bearing our sin, of which nakedness is a fitting
type. We have no covering for our iniquity apart from his
blood. "Naked, come to Thee for dress." Through grace,

we are robed with his righteousness. We are only too conscious of the fact that we have not adequately dealt with the perfect sufferings of our Lord, for none of the ransomed will ever know fully how dark the night was he passed through for our redemption. Sufficient, however, has been written to draw us nearer to his side, and to intensify our love, leading us to experience what Paul spoke of as "the fellowship of his sufferings" (Phil. 3:10). The apostle also describes how he bore in his body "the marks of the Lord Jesus" (Gal. 6:17).

Although we are not called upon to endure the torture, the physical pain and suffering he willingly faced, yet we must be willing to share his rejection and reproach. Ours must be a complete identification with our once smitten, now exalted and glorified Savior. As those bought with his blood, we must never forget that he died for us, and as his, we are crucified with him. How worthy he is to receive all we are and have, in virtue of all he surrendered for us! May we ever be found, therefore, giving him not lashes but love—not agony but adoration—not suffering, but submission—not humiliation, but honor! Until we see him as the Lamb slain from the foundation of the world, let us unfailingly plead his precious blood and rest in the glorious truth that—

> Jesus, my great High-priest,
>   Offered His blood and died;
> My guilty conscience seeks
>   No sacrifice beside;
> His powerful blood did once atone,
> And now it pleads before the throne.
>   *Isaac Watts*

Come, see the place where the Lord lay (Matt. 28:6).

16 /

Visiting the Grave

The Temple of heavenly blessing is founded upon the riven Rock, riven by the spear that pierced his heart. There is no scene in sacred history to gladden the soul like Calvary's dark tragedy. In life's sad hours, it is the thought of all Jesus endured that alleviates our sufferings and woes. As the poet expresses it:

> Is it not strange, the darkest hour
> That ever dawned on sinful earth
> Should touch the heart with softer power
> For comfort, than an angel's mirth?
> That to the Cross the mourner's eye should turn,
> Sooner than where the stars of Bethlehem shine.
> *Author Unknown*

In this meditation we are to think of his sweet resting place, when the agonies of the Cross were past. Visits to newly dug graves are solemn occasions, as we stand and remember our precious dead, and have heavenly, holy thoughts. After the death of a dear one visits to the grave are frequent. We often journey to God's green acre where the body of our loved one sleeps. This is why it is called *Cemetery,* which means, "the sleeping place," for there the precious dust will sleep until the resurrection morning. Time, however, is a wonderful healer, and as the days go by, visits to the grave grow less frequent, and as the years go by, the pilgrimage ceases.

We are to think, however, of the grave of graves, the place where the body of the Master lay for three days, awaiting a glorious resurrection. We cannot visit this sad yet fragrant place too often. God forbid that our journeys should grow less, until we forget his death for us. May we keep his grave ever fresh in our memories! Perhaps this is one reason why Jesus instituted the Memorial Feast, which is but a fresh visit to the grave, as we remember him.

What would we think of a bereaved wife who, after her husband's death, never went to his grave to silently remember her absent loved one? We would call her a callous, heartless widow, because by her action she proved the attachment between them not to be very deep or real. Yet there are those who profess to love the Lord who never remember his death in this appointed way, and his heart must be grieved.

No matter how we may try to wriggle out of the observance of the Lord's Supper, the fact remains that if a Christian fails to participate in the Feast when he is able, he is guilty of the positive sin of disobedience, for Jesus said, "This do in remembrance of me" (Luke 22:19). But, as in thought, we bow at the place where he was buried, several truths arise:

1. *It was a grave*

Jesus came and lived a human life, passed through human experiences, and had the usual end:

Low in the grave He lay,
Jesus my Saviour.
                                    Robert Lowry

The music of a baby's cry came from his lips, as did the moans of a dying man. He had a death, as well as a birth, a grave as well as a cradle, a shroud as well as swaddling clothes. But his was not a grave on a lonely, windswept moor as many a desert traveler and covenanter has found, but in a garden, bright with the flowers of spring, and decked with the beauties of nature. This may be where the custom arose of carrying flowers to a burial.

The garden grave of Jesus offers a parable of grace. If the One who was buried in such a lovely spot is accepted as Savior, he quickly changes our grave of sin and wilderness of despair into a garden of fragrant flowers. When we come to his grave, and allow him to bury our sin and self deep within it, we find the grave to be a garden. If as the kernel of wheat, we fall into the ground and die, we then bring forth fruits and flowers both beauteous and bountiful. We also have the pledge and pattern of resurrection here. If the grave represents *death,* the garden stands for victory over death. The One who was buried in a grave has a wonderful way of transforming graves into gardens.

2. *It was an empty grave*

Proclaim it yet once again to the nations that the true church is built upon an empty grave. The glorious truth is that those who loved Jesus found the grave empty when they visited it! "He is not here," said the angel. Our basic verse says, "Come, see the place where the Lord lay"— not lying. He was there, but broke the shackles, forsook the prison-house of death, for it had been declared, would not be "holden" of death (Acts 2:24). What a mournful creed is chanted in the lines

> Now He is dead! Far hence He lies
> In torn Syrian town;
> And on His grave with shining eyes
> The Syrian stars look down.
> *Matthew Arnold*

We much prefer the Christian Creed expressed in words:

> Up from the grave He arose!
> With a mighty triumph o'er His foes!
> He arose a Victor from the dark domain,
> And lives for ever with His saints to reign:
> He arose! He arose!
> Hallelujah! Christ arose.
> *Robert Lowry*

We cannot visit too often that empty grave, delight in it too ardently, revere it too solemnly, or declare it too loyally. Being an empty grave it preaches three sublime truths:

1. The Father was so well pleased with his beloved Son's sacrifice on our behalf that *he* raised him from the dead. Further, in virtue of his Son's death, God makes us welcome to his heart and home.

2. The empty tomb is the pledge to my soul of the risen life which the Risen Lord is able to bestow on me, through the power of his Spirit. But is this risen life fully realized and experienced by me?

3. It is a testimony that our faith is not in vain, and thus prophesies that one day all who sleep in Jesus will follow him into joy unspeakable and full of glory.

3. *It was a new grave*

Two phrases illustrate the fitting grave for the Lord of Glory: "Wherein never man before was laid" (Luke 23:53), and "His own new tomb" (Matt. 27:60). Thus, the One born in the womb of Mary is now buried in the virgin tomb of Joseph—a most becoming end for him who had lived a virgin life. Because he created all things, he is worthy of the first and the best, and the preeminence in all things unstained and untouched by man or sin. The colt that bore him into Jerusalem was one "whereon yet never man sat" (Luke 19:30; Mark 11:12). Having given the best for us, he expects the best from those redeemed by his blood.

Further, that new grave was befitting him who came to do a new thing in world history, namely, to conquer him that had the power of death, even the devil. By his death and resurrection, he made an end of sin and prepared us for everlasting righteousness. So the message of the empty but new grave is, "Behold, I make all things new." There had been countless thousands of graves, before his body reposed in Joseph's new tomb, but none so unique as the one who was God manifest in flesh.

4. *It was a borrowed grave*

When Jesus left the glory all he asked for was a stable to be born in, a Cross on which to die, and a spot to be buried in. So, "He made his grave with the wicked, and with the rich in his death" (Isa. 53:9). Most people have graves of their own to be buried in when they come to pass hence, unless they are buried in a pauper's grave. Such was his poverty that his body was laid to rest in another's grave—a climax to his life of humiliation. Although the Creator, he became dependent upon one of his creatures. Born in another's manger, dining at another man's table, sleeping in another's bed, he is now buried in another's tomb. Rich, for our sakes he became poor that we might be enriched forever by his grace. While here on earth, he had nothing of his own but was dependent upon God and man for what he needed. We greatly err if we count possessions as ours, failing to remember that he is the source of every precious thing. All we have is like the grave He was buried in—*borrowed!* "O Lord, the tomb is Thine, the rock forming it was fashioned by Thy power, the garden in which it was placed was kissed into beauty by Thy lips. Take it all. The cost of preparing it is nothing in comparison to that death of Thine. In giving Thee a grave, we but minister unto Thee of Thine own."

5. *It was a disciple's grave*

What a moving verse this is in connection with the entombment of Jesus: "When the even was come, there came a rich man of Arimathaea, named Joseph, who also himself was Jesus' disciple" (Matt. 27:57)! The composite portrait of Joseph drawn by the Four Evangelists indicates that he was a most commendable character.

Matthew gives us the Jewish ideal of him: "a rich man." Mark, the Roman ideal: "an honorable counselor." Luke, the Greek ideal: "a counselor good and just"; John, the divine ideal: "a disciple of Jesus." The tomb, then, was the property of this noble, generous, unselfish man, who had prepared it for his own burial. How he must have revered it after Jesus rose from the dead! This secret friend of Jesus revealed himself at the time of Christ's deepest dishonor, and by his gracious act of surrendering his grave, and lovingly preparing his body for burial, and delivering himself from secrecy, he declared to all that the One he loved was buried in his grave.

Is it not somewhat remarkable that Jesus was associated with two Josephs, one at either end of his short yet remarkable career? Joseph, his foster-father, was a poor laboring man, eking out a living as a carpenter. He gave him a home as he entered the world. Joseph of Arimathaea was a wealthy man who gave him a beautiful grave as he left the world, more lavish than the stable he was born in. Both lodged and befriended Jesus when he was despised and rejected by others. The first Joseph cared for him as an unwanted Babe for whom there was no room in the inn, and when with his mother, the family had to flee into Egypt. The other Joseph cared for him after he had been cruelly martyred, unwanted as a King, and sent out of the world as a felon.

Because he is still the unwanted One, Jesus yearns for more Josephs to give him a resting place. Is your heart one? He no longer requires a manger to be born in, or a tomb to be buried in. All sorrows and privations are past for him. But he desires that you should shield him in your heart as a home from the scorn of a bitter world. If others have no place for him, let us hide him as one Joseph did in his home, and the other in his grave.

17 /

That I may know him, and the power of his resurrection, and the fellowship of his sufferings, being made comformable unto his death (Phil. 3:10).

A Quartet of Resurrection Blessings

In the most wonderful, all-inclusive verse we have given under this meditation, Paul declares the resurrection as a *Fact* and *Factor* in his quartet of desires:

"That I may know him." The Apostle puts the adorable Person of his Lord first. He yearned for him before his works and possessions.

"The power of his resurrection." Paul sought to understand this truth, not theoretically, but experimentally. He wanted fellowship in it.

"The fellowship of his sufferings." Calvary and the empty tomb are linked together. If we are risen in him, we must be prepared to suffer for him. Paul entered deeply into these sufferings.

"Made comformable to his death." This implied the working out of the Cross in Paul's life and represents the death-principle in the self-life. What the Lord desires is not so much our *doing* as our *dying*. The *fact* of Christ's death and resurrection must become a *factor* in the disciple's experience. It is upon the second of this quartet of blessings that we are to dwell, thinking first of the Resurrection:

As a Fact: "His Resurrection"

We should carry in our minds a brief summary of all
that is involved in this most important doctrine of Scripture,
seeing it is one of the most glorious truths recorded in the
New Testament. The whole system of Christianity stands
or falls by it. Paul affirmed that "if Christ be not risen,
your faith is vain; ye are yet in your sins" (1 Cor. 15:17).
Once we admit the miracle of his resurrection, then all other
miracles recorded in the Gospels were possible. Modernism
casts doubt on the veracity of the statements about Jesus
rising from the dead, and its rejection of this fundamental
truth is to be deplored. With this denial comes the effort
to explain the miraculous in Scripture from a natural
standpoint.

The Resurrection is the subject of prophecy, for David
by the Spirit forecast of the Lord: "Thou wilt not leave
my soul in hell: neither wilt thou suffer thine Holy One
to see corruption" (Ps. 16:10)—a prophecy Peter related
to Jesus, when he affirmed that, with all the other apostles,
he witnessed his resurrection (Acts 2:30–32). Jesus himself
often spoke of, and implied, that he would rise again from
the grave. If this fact is denied, however, the truth of inspiration is nullified, for the prophets affirmed that the Holy
Spirit inspired them to set forth such a victory over death.
If he had no resurrection, then the prophets were liars for
they declared that God would raise up Christ.

The Resurrection was the constant theme of the early
church. They said of Paul that "he preached unto them
Jesus, and the resurrection" (Acts 17:18; cp. 24:15). Great
spiritual upheavals followed the preaching of the glorious
fact—and, adversely, the opposition of materialists. Although modern thought stops at "Jesus" and does not go
on to "and the resurrection," as the church proclaims the
full message she experiences resurrection results. That

Christ's victory over the grave was a reality, the existence of the church clearly proves. Her presence in the world substantiates such a fact. If he had no resurrection body, then there is no mystical body, for the Holy Spirit came to form such as the outcome of our Lord's resurrection and ascension. Every born-again believer is a living witness of this precious doctrine, as a dynamic in life. Through its power the ungodly are transformed into saints. They rise from their grave of sin because Jesus is alive forevermore.

Paul makes it clear that the Resurrection is vitally connected with the work of salvation in the individual soul, and is, therefore, of paramount importance. "If thou shalt . . . believe in thine heart that God hath raised him from the dead, thou shalt be saved" (Rom. 10:9). Thus, as it has been expressed:

"The Resurrection of Christ is the heart of Christianity which makes it pulsate with the life of God.

It is the keystone to the arch of truth which holds all the faith of the Gospel together.

It is the foundation of the Church—it is the mainstay of Christian activity.

It is the lever of power which shall move the world;

It is the link that unites all believers."

The story is told of a poor little London boy gazing into a store window in which was displayed a large picture of Jesus hanging on a Cross. As his small eyes were riveted on the scene, evidently his heart was moved. A gentleman passing by was attracted by the intense interest the boy was manifesting in the picture. Coming to his side he asked, "Who's that, and what's being done to that man hanging there?" In his typical cockney way the boy replied, "Don't yer know, sir, that's Jesus. Bad men took and hanged 'im there to die." "Terrible, terrible," said the man as he patted the boy on the head and continued his journey. Very soon, however, he heard feet pattering behind him. Turning he saw that it was the lad he had just left. "Well, what is it, boy?" he asked. Excitedly, the urchin said, "Forgot to tell yer, sir, they put 'im in a grave, but 'e got up again!" Let us not forget that he did get up again, that although once dead, he is alive forevermore.

Hallelujah! Christ arose!

As a Factor: "The *power* of his resurrection"

Weymouth translates the phrase, "The power which is in his resurrection." Paul was passionately keen to know and experience the amazing forces at work as the result of Christ's dominion over death. If only we could come into the sweep of this tremendous current, how uplifted we would be in their strength, as we are borne along the Christian pathway by their almighty power. Here are a few aspects of the power latent in his resurrection:

Power to Justify

Such risen, justifying power is of a twofold nature, namely, the Person of the Savior and the Position of the Sinner. The death of Christ proves the love of God: his resurrection displays the power of God to assist the sinner in every way.

Think of the justification of the Savior!

During his earthly life and ministry he made claims which astounded those around him, and which they stoutly discredited as, for instance, when he made himself equal with God (John 5:18). He declared himself "to be the Son of God with power . . . by the resurrection from the dead" (Rom. 1:4). Men sought to stone him for such an assertion, but his triumph over death proved his claim that he was the Son of God with power. Such a victory was an open manifestation and a seal of what he had described himself to be.

He was put to death as an impostor and a blasphemer, and given a felon's Cross—evidence of their estimation of him. But God raised him from the death to which cruel men condemned him. He justified all his words and works by the empty tomb, and, thereby proved that he was the righteous Lord. His loftiest claims were vindicated, and all doubts regarding his validity removed. Now—

> He breaks the power of cancelled sin,
> He sets the prisoner free;
> His blood can make the foulest clean,
> His blood availed for me.
> *Charles Wesley*

If the Cross was what men thought about Jesus, his resurrection was what God thought about him. What else can we do but bow in reverential homage, exercising adoring faith in what his rising again meant to him!

Think of the justification of the sinner!

The twin need of man is vitally associated with the twin work of Christ, as found in Paul's treatise on justification in Romans 4. "Who was delivered for our offences, and was raised again for our justification" (4:25).

1. *Delivered for our offences*

Jesus offered himself as a Sacrifice for the sins of the world, even for your "offences" and mine. He did not die for any offense of his own for "he was holy, harmless, undefiled, separate from sinners" (Heb. 7:26). But when he was raised again, the sinner was assured that God had accepted his Son's sacrifice on his behalf; that the Resurrection was God's receipt that man's debt had been paid. It was a convincing proof of the perfection and efficacy of the atonement his death procured. The design of his death was to put away sin, and his resurrection and exaltation declares that, through faith, our sin has been put away and will be remembered against us no more. If God had not been satisfied with the sacrifice of Christ on behalf of offenders, he would have kept their Substitute in his grave.

2. *Raised again for our justification*

In his justification of the Perfect Man, God provided a justification for the race of which the Risen Lord is the Head. As there is life in the root for all branches of a tree, so in Christ, raised from the dead, there is life for all. God draws near in the perfect Person of his Son and offers pardon to all who believe. He remains just, yet is the justifier of all who come to him by faith. Having no righteousness of our own, we come into an accepted position when united with the Righteous One. Through the death and resurrection of Jesus we have a righteousness, not of a perfected character, but of a rectified relationship. Now God regards us, not for what we are in ourselves, but what we are in Christ through our vital connection with him as our Righteous Head. Resting in him as the Risen Lord, we are delivered from the burden of guilt and sense of condemnation, for God will not require payment for our debt twice over.

POWER TO REVIVIFY

Paul's message to the Ephesians was, "You hath he quickened, who were dead in trespasses and sins" (2:1). "Quickened" means to make alive, to revivify, to be born again. Jesus rose for our justification, that we might be quickened together with him, in and through the regeneration by the Spirit. In sin man is spiritually dead, but by the power of the Spirit, in virtue of the death and resurrection of Jesus, he can be made alive. What a priceless privilege is ours to be one with the Man who snapped the bars of death and walked out of his tomb to an endless life. The power of the Resurrection is seen in the fact that no grave can hold us whether in bondage, or in moral or material corruption. Had there been no Resurrection, there would have been no regeneration, but now the Risen Lord operates by the Holy Spirit in the life of the soul. He was raised from the dead that "we also should walk in newness of life" (Rom. 6:4). Risen with him, ours is the obligation to seek those things which are above.

POWER TO UNIFY

The Resurrection possesses wonderful power in that it makes the believing soul one with Christ and also part of each other. It also makes possible the transference of our life from the earthly level to a heavenly sphere. *Positionally,* we have been placed in the heavenlies by the Resurrection, and nothing can affect our position there. It is ours for ever (Eph. 1:3, 20; 2:6). *Experimentally,* fellow-believers are one with the Lord below, as well as above. "Quickened together," we must be "knit together" (Col. 2:13, 19). When we allow what we are in him up in heaven to be translated by the Spirit into spiritual unity down here, then we prove the sanctifying power of the Resurrection in our unification with Christ, and with his own blood-washed children. We are all one in Christ Jesus.

POWER TO NULLIFY

Having defeated his enemy, the devil, the Risen One can conquer all enemies. What marvelous adulation Paul ascribed to him when he wrote, "Having spoiled principalities and powers, he made a show of them openly, triumphing over them in it" (Col. 2:15). Greater than the strong man, he revealed himself the conqueror of Satan in his own dominion. No longer has Satan the power of death. The injuries caused by the Fall are repaired, and sin can be nullified in your life and mine. "Because I live, ye shall live also" is the Risen Lord's pronouncement. Ours is a twofold salvation by Christ: a salvation from the guilt and penalty through his death, and a salvation from the government and power of sin through his resurrection. Paul had the latter in mind when he spoke about being "saved by his life," that is, his risen life. "To this end Christ both died, and rose, and revived, that he might be Lord both of the dead and *living*" (Rom. 14: 9).

Is he our Lord, practically? Are we bound to him in order that we might live unto him? He does not look for his risen ones in the dead things of the world. They are not there, but risen into a newness of life. Is this not the truth emphasized in our basic text when it speaks about conformity to his death? Through our association and intercourse with our precious Risen Lord, our whole nature is exalted to a higher plane. If habits and worldly desires are entwining themselves around our lives, and we long to be free, let us strive to know the power of his resurrection— a power emancipating us from sin's enticements, dropping from us as dead leaves from a tree.

> Buried with Christ, and raised with Him too;
> What is there left for me to do?
> Simply to cease from struggling and strife,
> Simply to walk in newness of life—
>   Glory be to God.
>
> *J. Ryder*

Power to Vivify

"Vivify" means to endue with life, and this is what will transpire when the dead in Christ are raised incorruptible, as Paul declares in his great resurrection chapter, 1 Corinthians 15. Although we might heartily sing, "The sky not the grave is our goal," we know, only too well, that if Christ does not return in our lifetime, and so translate us without dying, that a grave will be the goal of our bodies. But as the apostle clearly teaches, there is to be a resurrection of the dead, both of the just and the unjust (Acts 24:15, 21). "If there be no resurrection of the dead, then is Christ not risen" (1 Cor. 15:13, 35–50). There is to be a redemption of the body when he returns to "change our vile body, that it may be fashioned like unto his glorious body" (Phil. 3:21). This mortal dust laid in a grave is to be quickened by the Spirit (Rom. 8:11). The grave is not to have the final victory. When the Lord rose from the tomb and went to heaven with his uncorrupted, glorified, body, he displayed himself as the Conqueror of death, and as the representative of all his saints who will receive their spiritual body out of their buried dust, as at the beginning Adam received his natural body out of the dust of the earth.

At death, the whole man seems to perish, with no sign of revival, but Christ, by his resurrection, brought immortality to light. To believe this truth is to break the tyranny of death and make the future no more an adventure. Now, we do not think of the Father's home as a sphere of disembodied spirits, having no identity, for we have the assurance that the Spirit will transform our buried dust into a body like unto his own. Did he not say to those bereaved hearts in Bethany, "Thy brother shall rise again" (John 11:23)? This will be true of all who sleep in Jesus. May we go forth then, in these materialistic days, resting in the power of his glorious Resurrection, living not as weeping friends of a dead prophet but as heroic soldiers of the Prince of Life. May we be found as partners of him who could say, "I am he that liveth, *and was dead;* and, behold, I am alive for evermore" (Rev. 1:18).

*This do in remembrance of me
(Luke 22:19).*

18 /

*The Rosemary
of Remembrance*

Of all services associated with the worship within the
Christian church, the Lord's Supper is the most solemn,
impressive, and instructive. It is also the simplest, when
divested of the ceremonial trappings man has wrapped
around it. In its naked simplicity it is heart-moving. It is
called the Lord's Supper, or the Lord's Table, because it
was instituted by him as a means of commemorating his
supreme sacrifice for us. All connected with this Feast of
Faith, Hope, and Love centers around his adorable Person—"Remember *Me.*" In the upper room that night he
abolished the Passover Jewish Feast, representing, as it did,
the deliverance of Israel from death through the shed blood
of lambs. The sprinkled doorposts and lintels of the house-
holds of the Israelites in Egypt, and the feasting upon roasted
lamb was observed until Christ came and established the
Christian Feast proclaiming himself as the Passover sacrificed for us. All who partake of the Supper are, or should
be those sheltered by the blood of Jesus, for participation
implies salvation.

THE REQUEST: "This do"

These two words, *This do,* imply that we have no option but to obey. Paul added emphasis to the loving request when he said concerning the Supper, "I have received of the Lord" (1 Cor. 11:23). Attendance at the Table is not something we can please ourselves about, but it is imperative that we obey. Then behind these two words we can detect the order of this memorial Feast instituted and commanded by the Lord. The breaking and handling of the bread and drinking the wine are the simple means by which his death is kept before us. Knowing how apt the human mind is to forget, he chose the elements as sacred emblems and loving mementos, whereby we can keep fresh and green in our weak and forgetful memories all he accomplished for us.

It was Thomas Moore of the sixteenth century who gave us the sentence, "Memory breathes her vesper sigh to those taking our minds back to the past." This quaint poet also left us the lines:

> No, the heart that has truly loved
> never forgets,
> But as truly loves on to the close.
> *Thomas Moore*

Sitting at his table, as those who truly love him, we cannot forget the travail of soul. Vesper-sighs escape us as our Spirit-inspired minds take us back to Calvary where he died that we might be forgiven and made his own.

1. *The Command of a Lord*

There are those who profess to be the Lord's who deem his table to be unnecessary, and so have no place for it in their worship. Our obligation, however, is not to be influenced by the theories and thoughts of men, but to take the Lord's words as they stand. We have no specified command as to how often we should participate in the Feast. Paul's injunction is, "As oft as ye eat and drink," but he did not say how often. Many saints follow the apostolic practice of linking the Lord's Supper to the Lord's Day, and thus remember him weekly. Others observe it monthly or quarterly. It is not the frequency that counts but the spirit in which we participate. The very frequency some churches observe may have the tendency to beget a familiarity resulting in a cold, dead formalism. Further, to engage in such a holy service merely because we are commanded to do so is to rob it of its spiritual impact upon life. Loving him as our Lord, our obedience to his command results in blessing.

2. *The Request of a Friend*

We can also see in these words, "This do," the dying request of our heavenly Friend, of our Lover Divine. It is as if he said, in effect, "My body will soon be broken for you, and when I am gone do not forget me. Come together as often as possible, and as you partake of the bread and wine, remember me and all that I suffered for your sake." Remembrance on the human plane can help us to understand his request. A lock of hair can recall the love and goodness of a departed loved one as we fondly gaze at it. A little shoe hidden away in a drawer can recall to the heart of a parent, a baby, untarnished by sin, taken by death. As gifts cherished yet valueless in themselves (yet priceless to us) call to remembrance the dead who yet speak to our hearts, so the ordinary bread and wine are remembrance tokens.

In conversation with a friend, a young man drew out a letter from his sister in a distant land in which he had once lived. Disclosed were a pressed flower and a few green grass blades. Presenting them, the young man said with deep emotion, "These are from my mother's grave." So the cheap elements of the Supper are valueless in themselves, but yet priceless because they remind us of him who suffered and died in our place. They take us to Calvary, to the Savior's grave, and onward to glory. Thus, in partaking of the emblems we respect the wish of a dying Friend and obey the command of a loving Lord. As my Lord, he commands my presence at his table; as my Friend, he desires it.

> Remember Thee, and all Thy pains
> And all Thy love to me;
> Yea, while a breath, a pulse remains
> Will I remember Thee.
> *James Montgomery*

THE REMEMBRANCE: "In remembrance of me"

Let us now turn to think more fully of him who is the sole object of our remembrance, for his presence makes the Feast. We are exhorted to remember not only his words, works, and ways, but himself. "Remember Jesus Christ." We are not to fix our thoughts on the table or emblems. There is a tendency to think more of the Feast than the Friend—the Supper than the Savior. The emblems come before Emmanuel. We must, however, strive to make more of "the *Lord* of the Feast," rather than "the *feast* of the Lord"

ME—*The Lowly Nazarene*

The thoughts filling the minds of the disciples as they remembered their Lord in his appointed way would revolve around who and what he was in the days of his flesh. Since he was made in the likeness of a man, and fashioned as one, they would often recall his humanity, as bone of their bone, and flesh of their flesh—One so human yet divine.

The sacrament proclaims him as the man Christ Jesus, the Mediator. The bread tells us that he had a real, living body like our own. The wine indicates that, like us, he possessed warm, red blood, but unlike ours, his was untainted by sin.

ME—*The Crucified Savior*

His shame, suffering and sacrifice form the burden of the feast for it revolves around all he accomplished on the wondrous Cross on which he died. The broken bread suggests the bruises and pains his sacred body suffered through the nails that held him fast to the tree. The outpoured wine symbolizes the bitter cup he drank in which was his blood, so red, for sinners shed.

ME—*The Victorious Redeemer*

The early custom of linking together the Lord's Table and the Lord's Day provides a twofold view of the act of remembrance. The Supper calls us to think anew of his free grace, sacrificial death, and redemptive work. The Day bids us remember that he did not remain dead, but rose again, a Victor o'er the dark domain. "Delivered for our offenses"—sacrament aspect. "Raised again for our justification"—Sabbath aspect. When he instituted the Supper, Jesus did not specify *any particular day* on which observance should be undertaken.

ME—*The Ascended Lord*

In apostolic times when the church came together to engage in this holy love-feast, she would have vivid recollections of the last days the Savior spent on earth with his own. How the saints would also recall the stupendous miracle of his translation to heaven from Mount Olivet, when he led captivity captive, and yet rejoiced that he was with them presiding over the Feast.

ME—*The Interceding Advocate*

We cannot partake of the emblems and remember his past work without looking up and seeing him as our Great High Priest, interceding on our behalf in the holiest of all. The Cross is the foundation of his present ministry in heaven, where his five bleeding wounds pour effectual prayers for his church. So, as we remember him down here, he remembers us up there before the Father's face.

ME—*The Coming Bridegroom*

The Feast covers the journey of the Savior from his Cross to his Crown—from the Tree to the Throne. As we are drawn into the shadows of dark Calvary, the glory of the future bursts upon us in all its splendor, for as we eat and drink we remember the Lord's death—*till he come*. This is why true faith can sing:

> Feast after feast thus comes and passes by,
>   Yet passing points to that glad feast above.
> Giving sweet foretaste of the festal joy
>   The Lamb's great bridal feast of bliss and love.
>   *Horatius Bonar*

Between the calling out of the Jews from Egypt to the first coming of Christ, there was the one feast, the Passover associated with the Red Sea when under Moses a great deliverance was theirs. Between the calling out of the church at Pentecost, as the result of the Cross, to the second coming of Christ, there is another Feast, speaking of emancipation from the bondage of sin in the lives of those who participate. As the Feasts come and go, we should be learning to cultivate more perfectly the glory gaze, for the Table has two finger-posts—one pointing back to Calvary, "The Lord's death"; the other pointing forward to the coming Bridegroom, "Till he come."

I once read the story of a brilliant young doctor who had dedicated his career to the fighting and cure of a foul disease. He was engaged to be married to a charming young lady who was also a doctor. The two of them made a love-bargain that if he died before they wedded, that she would spend her life continuing his work. Alas! he fell a victim to the fatal disease he was fighting. Then came the test of love for the bereaved lover. After a while the loved one had many suitors offering her marriage, but she never gave her hand in marriage to any. Her reply to all was the same, *I am married to his remembrance.* What undying love and noble heroism she manifested in continuing her loved one's task!

As we think of Jesus and the Feast he instituted, do we emulate such an example of devotion? He is our sacrificial Lover who gave his life battling against the disease of sin, and he died on behalf of all smitten ones. Are we his unfailing partners in love's bargain to revere his memory, and to perpetuate his work? The world would seek to court us, craving for hand and heart, so that it might replace him to whom we are betrothed. When religious friends would seduce us away from actual participation in the memorial Feast, affirming that it is no longer necessary for us, we should earnestly entreat them to leave us alone, for Jesus is our absent Lover. Before he died, he lovingly requested us to remember him in his designed way. As those who love him we must comply with his request, and ever say to our hearts, *I am married to his remembrance!*

Bibliography

Abbott, Dean Eric. *The Compassion of God and the Passion of Christ.* London: Geoffrey Bles, 1963.

Berkhof, Louis. *Vicarious Atonement through Christ.* Grand Rapids: Wm. B. Eerdmans Co., 1936.

Burrell, David J. *The Wondrous Cross.* New York: American Tract Society, 1898.

Burrows, Winfrid O. *The Mystery of the Cross.* London: Rivingtons, 1912.

Clow, W. M. *The Cross in Christian Experience.* London: Hodder and Stoughton, 1908.

Durbanville, Henry. *The Last Words.* Edinburgh: B. McCall Barbour, 1954.

Fincayson, R. A. *The Cross.* London: Parry Jackman Ltd., 1955.

Fraser, Neil M. *The Grandeur of Golgotha.* London: Pickering and Inglis, 1959.

Fryhling, Paul P. *Steps to Crucifixion.* Grand Rapids: Zondervan Publishing House, 1961.

Green, Peter. *Watchers by the Cross.* New York: Longmans, Green and Co., 1934.

Golladay, R. E. *Lenten Sermons and Outlines.* Columbus: Lutheran Books, 1905.

Hutchings, W. F. *Aspects of the Cross.* London: Longmans, Green and Co., 1897.

Liddon, Canon F. *Passiontide Sermons.* London: Longmans, Green and Co., 1892.

Logsdon, S. Franklin. *Lingering at Calvary.* Largo, Florida: Logsdon Co., 1950.

Maltby, W. Russell. *Christ and His Cross.* London: Epworth Press, 1935.

Mantle, Gregory. *The Way of the Cross.* New York: George H. Doran Co., 1922.

Marsh, F. E. *Why Did Christ Die?* Grand Rapids: Zondervan Publishing House, n.d.

Matthews, W. R. *Seven Words.* London: Hodder and Stoughton, 1933.

Morgan, G. Campbell. *The Bible and the Cross.* London: Westminster Publishing Co., 1930.

Mortimer, Alfred G. *Meditations on the Passion.* New York: Longmans, Green and Co., 1903.

Papini, Giovanni. *The Story of Christ.* London: Hodder and Stoughton, 1928.

Rees, Paul. *The Radiant Cross.* London: Marshall, Morgan and Scott, 1949.

Reid, S. J. *Do Not Sin against the Cross.* Grand Rapids: Wm. B. Eerdmans Co., 1940.

———— *The Seven Windows.* Grand Rapids: Wm. B. Eerdmans Co. 1940

Rimmer, Harry. *Voices from Calvary.* Grand Rapids: Wm. B. Eerdmans Co., 1936.

Sauer, Erich. *The Dawn of World Redemption.* Grand Rapids: Wm B. Eerdmans Co., 1950.

Simpson, Herbert L. *Testament of Love.* London: Hodder and Stoughton, 1934.

Sherwood, James M. *The History of the Cross.* New York: Funk and Wagnalls, 1883.

Spurgeon, Charles Haddon. *Christ's Words from the Cross.* Grand Rapids: Zondervan Publishing House, 1961.

Stalker, James. *The Death of Jesus.* New York: George F. Doran, 1894.

Stevenson, Herbert F. *The Road to the Cross.* London: Marshall, Morgan and Scott, 1962.

Strauss, Lehman. The Day God Died. Grand Rapids: Zondervan Publishing House, 1965.

Stroud, William. *The Death of Christ.* New York: Appleton and Company, 1871.

Weatherhead, Leslie D. *Personalities of the Passion.* London: Hodder and Stoughton, 1941.

Wheeler, F. L. *The Stations of the Cross.* London: S.P.C.K., 1955.

Wyand, Fred B. *Pen Pictures of Passion Week.* Grand Rapids; Zondervan Publishing House, 1942.

Scripture Index